×

The University
of Lo

2 Bunhill Row
London
EC1Y 8HQ

msl

D1612829

Adva

The University of Law
Incorporating The College of Law

The University of Law, 2 Bunhill Row, London, EC1Y 8HQ
Telephone: 01483 216371 E-mail: library-moorgate@law.ac.uk

This book must be returned on or before the last date stamped below.
Failure to do so will result in a fine.

Birmingham ׀ Bristol ׀ Chester ׀ Guildford ׀ London ׀ Manchester ׀ York

The College of Law, Moorgate

M12586

Elgar Advanced Introductions are stimulating and thoughtful introductions to major fields in the social sciences and law, expertly written by some of the world's leading scholars. Designed to be accessible yet rigorous, they offer concise and lucid surveys of the substantive and policy issues associated with discrete subject areas.

The aims of the series are two-fold: to pinpoint essential principles of a particular field, and to offer insights that stimulate critical thinking. By distilling the vast and often technical corpus of information on the subject into a concise and meaningful form, the books serve as accessible introductions for undergraduate and graduate students coming to the subject for the first time. Importantly, they also develop well-informed, nuanced critiques of the field that will challenge and extend the understanding of advanced students, scholars and policy-makers.

Titles in the series include:

International Political Economy
Benjamin J. Cohen

International Conflict and Security Law
Nigel D. White

The Austrian School of Economics
Randall G. Holcombe

Comparative Constitutional Law
Mark Tushnet

Advanced Introduction to

International Conflict and Security Law

NIGEL D. WHITE

Professor of Public International Law,
University of Nottingham, UK

Elgar Advanced Introductions

Edward Elgar
Cheltenham, UK • Northampton, MA, USA

© Nigel D. White 2014

All rights reserved. No part of this publication may be reproduced, stored in a retrieval system or transmitted in any form or by any means, electronic, mechanical or photocopying, recording, or otherwise without the prior permission of the publisher.

Published by
Edward Elgar Publishing Limited
The Lypiatts
15 Lansdown Road
Cheltenham
Glos GL50 2JA
UK

Edward Elgar Publishing, Inc.
William Pratt House
9 Dewey Court
Northampton
Massachusetts 01060
USA

A catalogue record for this book
is available from the British Library

Library of Congress Control Number: 2013954343

ISBN 978 1 78100 741 9 (cased)
ISBN 978 1 78347 352 6 (paperback)
ISBN 978 1 78100 742 6 (eBook)

Typeset by Servis Filmsetting Ltd, Stockport, Cheshire
Printed and bound in Great Britain by T.J. International Ltd, Padstow

Contents

Preface

There are many general introductory texts on international law, though the subject is now so vast that they are impossibly thin (with certain exceptions, for example, Vaughan Lowe's *International Law*), or more compendious yet unwieldy (for example Malcolm Shaw's *International Law*). Within international law there are now developed legal regimes governing human rights, environmental law, trade law . . . and accompanying literature; but there are numerous ways of examining international law. One way would be to look at issues of jurisdiction or responsibility that are common to each area; another way would be to bring together substantive areas of international law that are intimately related but, because of their increasing complexity, have been subject to separate treatment in the literature. In this regard, there are separate, monograph or textbook, treatments of arms control, collective security, use of force, the law of armed conflict, post-conflict law or *jus post bellum* treatises, many of which are referenced in this work.

The idea behind this book is to bring together the legal regimes addressing the basic issue of regulating violence between states and increasingly within states, within a coherent and accessible introductory text. The intention, though, is not simply to provide readers with a set of 'rules' governing uses of force, armed conflicts and the various actors involved in collective security, since international law does not work in this way in such a highly politicised area of international relations. Instead, the normative frameworks that have been developed to shape political action are identified and analysed in terms of legitimacy and efficacy as well as legality. To quote Martti Koskenniemi: 'Legal argument is never deduction from self-evident rules. It always adds to our understanding of the law, and thus to the identity, objective, and principles of the community'.[1]

---

1 M. Koskenniemi, 'The Place of Law in Collective Security' (1996) 17 *Michigan Journal of International Law* 456 at 480.

Abbreviations

ABM	Anti-Ballistic Missile Treaty (1972)
AJIL	*American Journal of International Law*
AP	Additional Protocol 1977
ASEAN	Association of South Eastern Nations
ASIL	*American Society of International Law*
AU	African Union
BWC	Biological Weapons Convention (1972)
BYBIL	*British Yearbook of International Law*
CWC	Chemical Weapons Convention (1993)
DRC	Democratic Republic of Congo
ECtHR	European Court of Human Rights
ECR	European Court Reports
EJIL	*European Journal of International Law*
EU	European Union
GC	Geneva Convention 1949
IAEA	International Atomic Energy Agency
ICISS	International Commission on Intervention and State Sovereignty
ICJ	International Court of Justice
ICLQ	*International and Comparative Law Quarterly*
ICRC	International Committee of the Red Cross
ICTY	International Criminal Tribunal for the Former Yugoslavia
IHRR	International Human Rights Reports
ILC	International Law Commission
JCSL	*Journal of Conflict and Security Law*
MAD	Mutually Assured Destruction
MJIL	*Melbourne Journal of International Law*
NATO	North Atlantic Treaty Organisation
NGO	Non-governmental organisation
NNWS	Non-nuclear weapons state
NPT	Non-Proliferation Treaty (1968)
NWS	Nuclear weapons state
OAS	Organisation of American States

OAU   Organisation of African Union
ONUC   United Nations Operation in the Congo
OPCW   Organisation for the Prohibition of Chemical Weapons
OST   Outer Space Treaty (1967)
P5   Five permanent members of the Security Council
PMSC   Private Military and Security Company
PoW   Prisoner of War
PRIF   Peace Research Institute Frankfurt
R2P   Responsibility to protect
RIAA   Reports of International Arbitral Awards
START   Strategic Arms Reduction Treaty
UN   United Nations
UNDP   United Nations Development Programme
UNEF   United Nations Emergency Force
UNGA   United Nations General Assembly
WMD   Weapons of Mass Destruction

1 Basic conditions of peace and security

1.1 Introduction

Any number of facts could be given to show that we live in a very violent world. To pick a few – there are tens of thousands of weapons of mass destruction (WMD) currently in existence, there are hundreds of thousands of child soldiers engaged in conflicts around the globe, and trillions of dollars are spent annually by states on military establishments. Additional statistics on the numbers of soldiers, tanks, artillery, rockets, mines, warplanes, naval vessels, small arms and so on, would simply overwhelm the reader and would, in all likelihood, lead to a sober assessment of the state of humankind that it was intent on self-destruction. However, the instinct for survival, inherent in human nature, provides a powerful restraint on the use of these means of violence.

In order to ensure the survival of the planet, more specifically the system of international relations based on nation-states, states and other key actors naturally act to establish the basic conditions for the control of violence. Without controlling and containing violence in international relations it would not be possible to establish a viable international political and legal order. Overall, the aim of international law is to reduce the levels of violence between states, and increasingly within states and against civilian populations (the achievement of peace), by addressing existential threats to states, peoples and groups (the achievement of security).

Historically, peace has been equated to the absence of war; security was viewed as the security of states from aggression by other states; and international laws and structures, such as balances of power between states or alliances of states, have reflected this. However, as international laws and institutions have been strengthened in response to major ruptures of international peace, especially at the end of major conflicts, there has been a deepening of the international consensus on

1

what is meant by peace and security, to cover sustainable peace within and between states, and the security of groups and individuals as well as states. Having said that, it is true to say that international law remains based on state security, reflected in fundamental inter-state compacts, and has been reinforced by a continued state-based monopoly on the means of using force. However, changes in the understanding of state sovereignty mean that it is no longer absolute; rather it is qualified by a responsibility towards civilian populations. This chapter will consider the concepts of peace and security that underpin the rules of international law in this most important area of international law, as well as the notions of sovereignty and statehood, which are central to it.

1.2   Understanding peace

Intuitively, peace is the antithesis of war. Peace should be the normal human condition and war the exception if our basic premise about the survival instinct remains true. However, by the nineteenth century a condition of war was seen as a valid alternative (not an exception) to peace. International law reflected and, indeed, secured this position containing separate regimes for the law of peace governing peaceful relations between states, and the law of war governing the relations between warring as well as neutral states. As Stephen Neff explains: 'War and peace were therefore, in a manner of speaking, inverse legal worlds – moral and legal looking glass images of one another'.[1]

The same act of violence, if carried out in a time of war, would be seen as a 'deed of heroic patriotism',[2] while in times of peace it would be treated as an international crime. A private ship and its crew commissioned by a government to attack enemy shipping during a war would be seen as a legitimate privateer, but during times of peace would be seen as pirates and, as such, *hostes humani generis* (the enemies of mankind).[3] The division into war and peace in international law has broken down to a great extent in modern times, although its influence remains.

---

1   S. Neff, *War and the Law of Nations* (Cambridge University Press, 2005) 177.

2   *Ibid.*, 178.

3   J.P. Grant and J.C. Barker, *Parry and Grant Encyclopaedic Dictionary of International Law* (3rd edn, Oxford University Press, 2009) 468; J.E. Thompson, *Mercenaries, Pirates and Sovereigns* (Princeton University Press, 1994) 43.

Sociological understandings of peace are probably more useful at this stage than legal definitions (which, in any case, tend to focus on 'war' or 'armed conflict'), as the aim of this chapter is to understand the purposes of the law – to understand peace and security as public goods, which the law is intended to help achieve.[4] The most influential approach in this respect is that of Johan Galtung, who defined peace as the absence of 'structural violence'. Structural violence is violence that is 'built into the structure' of society and 'shows up as unequal power and consequently as unequal life chances'.[5] It follows that in order to understand structural violence and the causes of war, issues of development, equality and, more broadly, social justice, have to be considered. This in turn leads to a broader definition of peace as consisting not only of the absence of war or other forms of structural violence but also having a positive aspect, defined by Galtung in terms of the 'integration of human society'.[6] Only the achievement of both negative and positive peace will ensure human survival and human flourishing.

Galtung's hugely influential work on peace is 'premised upon the identification of two global empirical tendencies that undermined the widespread image of an anarchical world order condemned to a perpetual condition of anticipating war'.[7] The first is that 'humans display a capacity for mutual empathy and solidarity' so that integration rather than disintegration is the natural state. The second is that humans show a capacity for restraint in the use of violence so they do not use the whole of their destructive capacity.[8] Both these tendencies are reflected in the often quite technical rules found in the law of armed conflict,[9] which limit the use of violence, both in terms of weapons used and targets chosen, both in international and, more recently, in internal armed conflicts. Although honoured more in the breach, the normativity of the law of armed conflict is not questioned (at least by states). Indeed, since the end of the Cold War in 1989, the first signs of more consistent enforcement of the law of armed conflict at the international level were the creation of *ad hoc* international criminal tribunals for Yugoslavia in 1993 and Rwanda in 1994, and the International Criminal Court

---

4 N. Tsagourias and N.D. White, *Collective Security: Theory, Law and Practice* (Cambridge University Press, 2013) chapter 2.

5 J. Galtung, 'Violence, Peace and Peace Research' (1969) 6 *Journal of Peace Research* 167 at 171.

6 J. Galtung, 'An Editorial' (1964) 1 *Journal of Peace Research* 1–4.

7 P. Lawler, 'Peace Studies' in P.D. Williams (ed.), *Security Studies: An Introduction* (Abingdon: Routledge, 2008) 73 at 82.

8 *Ibid.*, 82.

9 Reviewed in Chapter 6.

in 1998, with jurisdiction over war crimes, as well as crimes against humanity, genocide and (eventually) aggression.[10]

Galtung's premises accord with Herbert Hart's influential conceptualization of law as having a core content of natural law, which was endemic in the human condition, thereby preventing society from becoming a 'suicide club'.[11] Hart reasoned that 'without such a content laws and morals could not forward the minimum purpose of survival which men have in associating with each other'.[12] Such laws reflect the basic human conditions of vulnerability, approximate equality, limited altruism ('men are not devils dominated by a wish to exterminate each other'), limited resources, limited understanding and strength of will.[13]

Of course this still leaves the issue of how to achieve peace. Galtung's view was that peace had to be achieved by peaceful means,[14] reflecting a profound commitment to non-violence. Galtung's underlying, and powerful, premise for this position was that it is impossible to break the cycle of structural violence that is found within society (whether national or international) by violent means; thus ruling out even humanitarian forms of intervention designed to stop egregious structural violence within a state. However, international conflict and security law does not (yet) reflect Galtung's concept of peace. Although international law has developed to prohibit the use of force in international relations (the *jus ad bellum*),[15] the *jus ad bellum* does allow for exceptions, which, arguably, have been extended by practice. Moreover, international law does recognise the reality of conflict by having extensive rules on the conduct of hostilities during an armed conflict (the *jus in bello* or the law of armed conflict).

1.3 Understanding security

Drawing on the work of the Copenhagen School, security is the absence of existential threats against states, other security actors,

---

10 R. Cryer, 'War Crimes' in N.D. White and C. Henderson (eds), *Research Handbook on International Conflict and Security Law* (Cheltenham: Edward Elgar Publishing, 2013) 467.

11 H.L.A. Hart, *The Concept of Law* (Oxford: Clarendon, 1961) 188.

12 *Ibid.*, 189.

13 *Ibid.*, 190–93.

14 J. Galtung, *Peace by Peaceful Means: Peace, Conflict, Development and Civilisation* (London: Sage, 1996).

15 See Chapter 3.

peoples and individuals.[16] As with narrow conceptions of peace, the development of international relations to encompass collective security and human security has not meant that state security is no longer important. Realist visions of security focus on national security, in other words the safety of the nation-state, which necessitates placing national interests over collective interests, and thereby national security over collective security and human security.[17] Indeed, this vision of security is still strong, and has survived the Cold War confrontation between two heavily armed superpowers. Several explanatory factors can be pointed to. Firstly, states clearly still represent threats to other states, particularly those possessing nuclear weapons or other WMD. Secondly, what were once mainly domestic threats, such as terrorism, have become transnational, and, more generally, globalisation has led to internal security-focused politics becoming increasingly externalised.[18] Thus, national security issues are increasingly played out on a global scale, evidenced by the terrorist attack on the United States (US) of 11 September 2001, which led the US to wage a 'war on terror', more specifically a war against al-Qaeda, impacting around the globe.

Nonetheless, despite the continuing strength of national security, the concept of security has not only widened to include non-military threats such as those arising from food or environmental insecurity, but has also deepened to encompass human security.[19] Richard Falk defines 'security' as the 'negation of insecurity as it is specifically experienced by individuals and groups in concrete situations'.[20] The focus of international debate is increasingly on human security, which has been defined to include 'economic, environmental, social and other forms of harm to the overall livelihood and well-being of individuals'.[21] Clear evidence of the widening understanding of security is found in the pivotal post-Cold War United Nations (UN) Security Council summit held in January 1992. As an organ that is built on realist foundations, requiring agreement amongst its five permanent members (China, France, Russia, the United Kingdom (UK) and the US) for any substantive decision, the UN Security Council had previously almost

---

16 B. Buzan, O. Waever and J. de Wilde, *Security: A New Framework for Analysis* (Boulder: Lynne Rienner, 1998) 5.

17 H. Morgenthau, *Politics Among Nations* (New York: A. Knopf, 1972) 973.

18 P. Hough, *Understanding Global Security* (Abingdon: Routledge, 2008) 2.

19 *Ibid.*, 8.

20 R. Falk, *On Humane Governance: Toward a New Global Politics* (Cambridge: Polity, 1995) 147.

21 F.O. Hampson, 'Human Security' in P.D. Williams (ed.), *Security Studies: An Introduction* (Abingdon: Routledge, 2008) 229 at 231.

exclusively concerned itself with state and military security, but at its summit declared that the 'absence of war and military conflicts amongst States does not itself ensure international peace and security'; and that 'non-military sources of instability in the economic, social, humanitarian and ecological fields have become threats to peace and security'.[22]

As noted by Don Rothwell, the 'traditional view of security defines it in military terms with the primary focus on state protection from threats to national interests', but with the end of the Cold War 'security discourse has expanded beyond the traditional military domain with the proliferation of security agendas including economic security, environmental security, food security, bio-security, health security and human security'.[23] As recorded by Hitoshi Nasu, during the Cold War 'national security from external military attacks and threats was recognised as the ultimate raison d'etre of sovereign states',[24] although the Security Council supplemented this with the concept of international security, especially in the post-Cold War period and its authorisation to coalitions of willing states to undertake military actions to deal with threats to international peace as well as acts of aggression.

Attempting to understand security as a fixed concept fails to reflect how security has become a central feature of daily life. Rather security should be understood, according to the Copenhagen School, as a 'shared understanding of what is considered a threat'.[25] As Ronald Dannreuther explains, this reflects the turn towards 'constructivism' in the theorisation of security, 'with its focus on subjective ideas and intersubjective understandings', which 'accords a greater weight of how ideas and perceptions influence and structure international reality'.[26] The constructivist approach of the Copenhagen School shifts 'attention away from an objectivist analysis of threat assessment to the multiple and complex ways in which security threats are internally

22 Security Council Summit Statement Concerning the Council's Responsibility in the Maintenance of International Peace and Security, 31 January 1992, UN Doc S/23500 (1992).

23 D.R. Rothwell, K.N. Scott, and A.D. Hemmings, 'The Search for Antarctic Security' in A.D. Hemmings, D.R. Rothwell and K.N. Scott (eds), *Antarctic Security in the Twenty-First Century: Legal and Policy Perspectives* (Abingdon: Routledge, 2012) 1 at 3.

24 H. Nasu, 'Law and Policy for Antarctic Security' in Hemmings et al, *supra* note 23, 18 at 19.

25 *Ibid.*, 25; Buzan, Waever and de Wilde, *supra* note 16, 23–6.

26 R. Dannreuther, *International Security: The Contemporary Agenda* (Cambridge: Polity, 2007) 40.

generated and constructed'.[27] Furthermore, the Copenhagen School moves the study of security away from the narrow confines of the realist neo-scientist, 'rationally calculating the multiple security threats', towards a more democratic construction of security based on shared understandings found in organisations, governments, civil society and other non-state actors, including individuals.[28]

The Copenhagen School identifies those objects that are existentially threatened as 'referent objects'.[29] The referent object for security has 'traditionally been the state and, in a more hidden way, the nation'. This signifies that 'for a state, survival is about sovereignty, and for a nation, it is about identity'. However, following the constructivist approach 'securitizing actors can attempt to construct anything as a referent object'.[30] Thus, for the Copenhagen School, the 'referent object' is traditionally the state, although with new security agendas developing all the time the object can be collective concepts such as the environment or regions such as the Antarctic; and this is reflected in the UN Security Council's expansion of the concept of threat.[31] The ideas behind the terminology are very helpful in understanding the fact that security has expanded, though it is still state-centric, and that it is best understood through a constructivist lens as being based on inter-subjective understandings within legitimate security communities such as the UN Security Council and General Assembly.

1.4   Control and monopoly over the use of force

Both conditions of peace and security depend upon the control of violence in international relations. Uncontrolled violence signifies that, if law is present at all, it is largely an apology for violent conduct and not a means of regulating it. Furthermore, uncontrolled violence means that other legal orders that depend upon peace and security, that guarantee human rights and human flourishing, cannot be sustained. In this sense the law governing peace, regulating conflict and providing security (labelled in this book as international conflict and security law) is a pre-requisite to other international legal orders.

---

27 *Ibid.*, 42.
28 *Ibid.*
29 Buzan, Waever and de Wilde, *supra* note 16, 36.
30 *Ibid.*
31 Nasu, *supra* note 24, 25–6.

As we have seen, both peace and security are state-centric concepts: peace is primarily a condition between states and within states; and security is the absence of threat against states and other referent objects. International conflict and security law remains based on strong conceptions of statehood and sovereignty, but it has moved over the centuries towards regulating violence and force, first internationally and, in more recent times, within states. Nevertheless, generally in international relations theory a strong understanding of sovereignty persists, premised upon states having a continued monopoly over the use of force.

For Hans Morgenthau, a sovereign is the 'centralized power that exercised its law-making and law-enforcing authority within a certain territory'; a power that was 'superior to the other forces that made themselves felt in that territory'. According to Morgenthau, within a century after the Peace of Westphalia in 1648, the sovereign 'became unchallengeable either from within the territory or without . . . it had become supreme'.[32] The historical evidence presented in Chapters 3 and 4 suggests that this does not fully take account of the use of private violence for public purposes but, by the twentieth century, the state's monopoly over the use of force had been established. Thus, in 1918 Max Weber defined the modern state as a 'human community that (successfully) claims the monopoly of the legitimate use of physical force within a given territory'.[33]

According to Elke Krahmann, the state's internal monopoly on the legitimate use of force dates back to the seventeenth century; embodied in the social contract theory of Thomas Hobbes whereby citizens give up their right to use force in return for protection by the state.[34] In terms of the external use of force, states more gradually asserted control, and reduced their dependency (in the seventeenth and eighteenth centuries) on private violence (mercenaries, privateers and chartered companies).[35]

By the beginning of the twentieth century strong sovereignty was embodied in national citizen armies and increasingly sophisticated weaponry under absolute state control. State organs and state agents

---

32 Morgenthau, *supra* note 17, 306.

33 M. Weber, 'Excerpts from Politics as a Vocation', in C. Lemert (ed.), *Social Theory: The Multicultural and Classic Readings* (Boulder, Colo.: Westview, 1999) 111.

34 E. Krahmann, 'Private Security Companies and the State Monopoly on Violence: A Case of Norm Change?' (2009) 88 *PRIF-Reports* 2.

35 See Chapter 4.

prosecuted wars and states controlled the means of violence both externally and internally. Nevertheless, even in the era of 'War and Peace' in the nineteenth and early twentieth centuries, states agreed that even in times of war the devastating effects of total war were to be limited by the law of armed conflict (the *jus in bello*). Furthermore, the effects of the two world wars in the twentieth century led to regulation of when states could resort to force (the *jus ad bellum*), culminating in the prohibition on the use of force in the UN Charter. States' external monopoly on the use of force was thus restricted to self-defence, while the authority to use force to enforce peace was centralised in the UN Security Council. Although states no longer had the monopoly over when force could be used externally, they still possessed the means of violence so that if the UN Security Council wanted to authorise force, it would have to call upon states to deploy their armies in defence of the values of peace and security.

States' internal monopoly on the use of force has proved much more resistant to regulation by international law; until recent times, internal sovereignty was not seen as the proper subject matter for international regulation. International law was confined to laws governing relations between states – the law of nations. Ballard defines the state as having two main characteristics; firstly, 'as a sovereign it refuses to share its functions with others and concentrates them into its own hands'; and secondly, 'it exercises its power over those who live within its distinguishable borders'.[36] However, as argued by Huntington, with globalisation increasing the openness of states, states are no longer in control of flows of money, peoples, technology, goods and ideas. Thus, sovereignty has become permeable and reflects the 'emergence of a varied, complex, multi-layered international order more closely resembling' the pre-Westphalian period.[37]

This loosening of strong conceptions of sovereignty has led to an increasing focus on controlling excessive violence within states. Internally, violent states may not be any more likely to be externally violent, but the instability created by their internal destruction, generating transborder instability (with flows of refugees, armed

---

36 K.M. Ballard, 'The Privatization of Military Affairs: A Historical Look into the Evolution of the Private Military Industry' in T. Jager and G. Kummel (eds), *Private Military and Security Companies* (Wiesbaden: Verlag, 2007) 37 at 39.

37 S.P. Huntington, *The Clash of Civilizations and the Remaking of World Order* (New York: Touchstone, 1996) 35.

groups and the forces of other states) will undermine inter-state peace and security. Thus, controlling internal violence protects both human security – by attempting to address existential threats to populations and groups – and state security – by mitigating the transborder effects of internal violence.

1.5   Purposes of international conflict and security law

Peace and security can only be achieved by reducing the occurrence of violence between and within states. Even when conflict breaks out, violence should not be unregulated. States' retention of their monopoly on the means of using force signifies that excesses may occur both internally as well as externally, but, if states' power is regulated and channelled, there is the prospect of being able to enforce the peace, and to protect states and populations from existential threats to their security. It follows from this examination of the basic conditions of peace and security that we can tentatively identify the underlying purposes of international conflict and security law.

1.   Arms control. The aim is to control the spread of the means of violence. At its most basic arms control law involves the restriction, if not prohibition, of WMD (in order to prevent a global suicide club emerging). More ambitiously, international law aims at the regulation of the level of arms globally in order to enable states to maintain their internal and external sovereignty, and, increasingly, to limit the egregious effects on the civilian population of the use of certain weapons.

2.   Limit resort to force by states. The aim of international law (the *jus ad bellum*) is to regulate the use of force between states in order to protect state sovereignty and, increasingly, to enable peoples to achieve self-determination free from external intervention.

3.   Limit private violence. History shows that uncontrolled private violence within states, but also externally, undermines both peace and security. International law aims to regulate and control its usage.

4.   Tackle existential threats. The aim of international law is to address threats to states, peoples and groups of individuals coming from states, within states, from non-state actors and from non-military sources such as global warming.

5. Collectivise security. In order to prevent powerful states exter-
    nalising their national security concerns, institutions are created
    by international agreement in order to achieve collective security.
    International institutions develop shared understandings of peace
    and security and facilitate the protection of these values as well
    as developing normative frameworks within which they are to be
    achieved.

6. Limit the effects of warfare. International law is made by states and
    is, therefore, pragmatic in recognising the reality that in a world of
    limited resources, inequalities between states and artificial bound-
    aries, states will abuse their monopoly on violence and conflicts
    will occur. Although the condition of peace has (temporarily) been
    displaced, international law should not only facilitate the return to
    peace but should continue to protect human security during the
    period of hostilities.

7. Ensure post-conflict transition from war to peace. The regula-
    tion of post-conflict situations between states and within states
    is essential to ensure the stability of international relations and to
    provide for sustainable peace, as well as state and human security.

8. Protect peace and justice. International law aims to secure free-
    dom from conflict and threat, and, increasingly, to provide jus-
    tice between states and within states, so that the stability of states
    is deeper than that which is provided by effective control of the
    monopoly on violence. Post-conflict states should not simply
    be rebuilt on the basis of effective government, but on the basis
    of accountable, representative government. In general terms,
    legitimate governments are effective governments.

International conflict and security law has emerged to achieve these
purposes but, as Plato rightly recognised in the *Laws*,[38] law is an imper-
fect instrument of governance, an inherent defect that is exacerbated
in the instance of international law by the complexity of negotiations
and political compromise that goes into its formation. Thus, this book
aims to assess the progress international law has made towards the
purposes identified above by tackling them broadly in the order listed.

---

38 Plato, *Laws* (translated by T.J. Saunders, London: Penguin, 1976) 184–5.

2 Arms control law

2.1 Introduction

It was argued in Chapter 1 that the human survival instinct prevents most individuals from embarking on actions that could lead to their own destruction. Of course they may make misjudgements, but if humankind were driven in general by desire for destruction, we would not be here. Scaling this proposition up to the level of governments and states may seem simplistic, but even the most pragmatic and realist approaches to international law and international relations (for example, in the writings of Glennon and Waltz) recognise that states act out of self-interest and at the core of that is the survival of the state.[1]

The doctrine of Mutually Assured Destruction (MAD) that prevailed during the Cold War represented the bottom line for states' desire for survival. In the period when MAD prevailed each superpower was restrained from using their WMD in the sure knowledge that such a precipitate action would not only lead to the destruction of their enemy but to their own destruction. States may make serious, even catastrophic, misjudgements about what they can achieve militarily – France's invasion of Russia in 1812, Germany's invasion of the Soviet Union in 1941 and Iraq's invasion of Kuwait in 1990 each come to mind – but generally their survival instinct leads to more conservative calculations. Included in those calculations is some measure of arms control, especially of the most destructive weapons. Even during a period when there was an arms race between the superpowers, it was still possible to achieve some consensus on limiting the proliferation of WMD.

---

1 K. Waltz, *Theory of International Politics* (New York: Addison-Wesley, 1979) 186; M. Glennon, *The Fog of Law: Pragmatism, Security and International Law* (Stanford University Press, 2010) 53, 225.

2.2   Non-proliferation of WMD

A central plank in ensuring the survival of states is to prevent the spread of weapons that have the potential to destroy nations and peoples.[2] To achieve this, international law has, in part, qualified one of the basic principles of international law – that of sovereign equality. As well as dominating universal security institutions, the major powers (the five permanent members of the Security Council – the P5) have established their domination of security concerns in relation to the most powerful WMD – the nuclear weapon.

In general, the approach of the major powers and other states to WMD has been varied; banning chemical and biological weapons, while allowing certain states to retain nuclear weapons. The three principal non-proliferation treaties are the 1968 Nuclear Non-Proliferation Treaty (NPT), the 1972 Biological Weapons Convention (BWC) and the 1993 Chemical Weapons Convention (CWC). Despite the role of the International Atomic Energy Agency (IAEA) in the implementation of the NPT, and the Organisation for the Prohibition of Chemical Weapons (OPCW) in the implementation of the CWC, these treaties are dominated by states. The IAEA and OPCW help states achieve their basic goal of non-proliferation of WMD.

In general terms, the overall purpose of these treaties is to address the 'horizontal' proliferation of WMD to states that currently do not possess them. The treaties set out to do this by 'proscribing possession, development, and transfer of both single-use WMD-related materials (in other words, those items and technologies primarily suited for use in WMD development programs) as well as dual-use WMD-related materials (in other words, items and technologies which have both civilian and military applications)'.[3] As well as aiming to prevent the proliferation of WMD among a wider group of states, the treaties also aim to prevent the proliferation of weapons within states already possessing them (so-called 'vertical' proliferation).[4]

---

2 M. Sossai, 'Disarmament and Non-proliferation' in N.D. White and C. Henderson (eds), *Research Handbook on International Conflict and Security Law* (Cheltenham: Edward Elgar Publishing, 2013) 41.

3 D.H. Joyner, *International Law and the Proliferation of Weapons of Mass Destruction* (Oxford University Press, 2009) xv.

4 *Ibid.*

Given that both the regulation of violence and the means of violence are endemic in any society, these agreements are clearly foundational in that they purport to regulate the most dangerous forms of weapons, capable of facilitating the most violent and destructive international acts, and causing the most egregious harm to populations and their environment. The three treaties are by no means without numerous weaknesses – the NPT in particular was not meant to be the final say in the regulation of nuclear weapons[5] – but together they represent the building blocks upon which non-proliferation is built.[6]

In an influential article written at the time of the adoption of the NPT, Mason Willrich expressed little doubt about the significance of the treaty for achieving the 'goal of overriding importance in the nuclear era . . . the avoidance of nuclear war'.[7] The NPT was agreed in the Cold War period when both superpowers wished to draw back from the possibility of MAD, and should be seen in the context of other treaty developments, such as the Outer Space Treaty (OST) of 1967, which not only constituted a bargain between the superpowers on the usage and development (and demilitarisation) of outer space, but also was law-making for the rest of the international community. Of course the lineage of the NPT and OST can be traced back to the UN Charter, which, like the NPT and the OST, had at its heart a bargain between the major powers but was also binding on the wider community of states.

Arms control law includes a number of significant bilateral, contractual treaties concerning WMD or their means of delivery, exemplified by the now defunct Anti-Ballistic Missile (ABM) Treaty of 1972, and an on-going process of Strategic Arms Reduction Treaties (START) between the US and the USSR/Russia. In these treaties the terms of the agreement were hammered out on a take it or leave it basis by the two parties. The reciprocal rights and duties are relatively clear and, therefore, can be successfully implemented unless both parties agree on changes, or, as with the ABM Treaty between the US and USSR/Russia, one party withdraws. The ABM Treaty was the 'cornerstone

---

5 M. El Baradei, 'Towards a Safer World', *The Economist*, 16 October 2003, cited in Joyner, *supra* note 3, 68.

6 Joyner, *supra* note 3, xv. See further N.D. White, 'Interpretation of Non-Proliferation Treaties' in D.H. Joyner and M. Roscini (eds), *Non-Proliferation Law as Special Regime* (Cambridge University Press, 2012) 87.

7 M. Willrich, 'The Treaty on Non-Proliferation of Nuclear Weapons: Nuclear Technology Confronts World Politics' (1968) 77 *Yale Law Journal* 1447 at 1449.

of strategic stability' during the Cold War,[8] but it reflected the bilateral and bipolar nature of the Cold War;[9] hence its demise when that period of international relations ceased. Such treaties contribute to the achievement of security goals, but the underlying stability in a world full of dangerous weapons is provided by the NPT, the CWC and to a lesser extent the BWC.

2.3   Nuclear non-proliferation

The NPT of 1968 is commonly described as a 'grand bargain' between nuclear weapon states (NWS) and non-nuclear weapons states (NNWS).[10] This suggests some sort of exchange of rights and duties between these two different groupings of states. Essentially, NWS are obliged not to provide WMD to NNWS, and not to proliferate their own; indeed the obligation is to 'eventually disarm themselves of nuclear weapons'.[11] NNWS, on their side, agree not to acquire nuclear weapons or to develop them themselves. 'In exchange for their commitment to forgo what would otherwise be their right, equal to that' of NWS, NNWS insist on a right not only to acquire 'nuclear technologies for the purpose of civilian power generation', but also to recognise a duty on NWS to help in the development of the civilian nuclear programmes of NNWS.[12] In other words, the deal was for NWS to retain their right to nuclear weapons, while NNWS gave up any right to have them. In exchange for this departure from sovereign equality, NWS promised to disarm gradually and to help develop peaceful uses of nuclear technology in NNWS.

Although the NPT can be analysed as a contractual-type treaty, involving an exchange of rights and duties between states, it is arguable that the NPT is of a more fundamental contractual nature than many such treaties. In addition to those contracts that facilitate ordinary exchanges, there are those contracts that represent an agreement upon which a society is built, for instance, by limiting the rights and freedoms for members in exchange for strong government and security

---

8 J. Rhinelander, 'The ABM Treaty – Past, Present and Future (Part I)' (2001) 6 *JCSL* 91 at 92.

9 R. Mullerson, 'The ABM Treaty: Changed Circumstances, Extraordinary Events, Supreme Interests and International Law' (2001) 50 *ICLQ* 509 at 509.

10 Glennon, *supra* note 1, 129.

11 Joyner, *supra* note 3, 8.

12 *Ibid.*, 9.

(according to Hobbes),[13] or stronger freedoms and rights of members in exchange for a more liberal form of government and less security (according to Locke).[14] These 'social contracts' are more profound than a contractual transaction whereby one party agrees to give up weapons if the other party does (as in the START Treaties), or whereby one party agrees to come to the aid of another if attacked, as long as other parties will come to their aid if they are attacked (as in the North Atlantic Treaty Organisation (NATO) treaty).

Social contracts at the domestic level are embodied in constitutional documents, such as the Magna Carta of 1215 or the Bill of Rights 1689, when the English monarchy agreed to certain limitations upon their powers in exchange for loyalty; while at the international level they can be found in the UN Charter, whereby the five major powers agreed to act as the world's police force in exchange for voting rights (in the form of the veto) that no other member possessed. It is no coincidence that those five permanent members are the NWS at the heart of the NPT grand bargain, supporting the argument that the NPT is something more profound than an ordinary contractual-type treaty, since it develops the grand bargain found in the UN Charter by extending the inequality between the P5 and other states in matters of international security.

Although the treaty was originally adopted for twenty-five years, it was renewed indefinitely by consensus at the Review Conference in New York in 1995. Nevertheless, the three pillars of the bargain have come under pressure, with the US, for example, putting greater emphasis after 2001 on preventing the spread of nuclear weapons over its own obligations to disarm and to help with the development of peaceful uses of nuclear technology.[15] The final document of the 2010 NPT Review Conference put equal emphasis on each of the three pillars of the NPT: non-proliferation, the development of peaceful uses of nuclear energy, and disarmament by nuclear powers,[16] which witnessed a return to consensus in arms control under the influence of President Obama. It seems that there are clear indications that the grand bargain underpinning nuclear weapons is set to continue.

---

13 T. Hobbes, *Leviathan* (first published 1651, edited by J. Gaskin, Oxford University Press, 1988).

14 J. Locke, *Two Treatises on Government* (first published 1690, edited by P. Laslett, 3rd edn, Cambridge University Press, 1988).

15 D.H. Joyner, *Interpreting the Nuclear Non-Proliferation Treaty* (Oxford University Press, 2011) 35.

16 *Ibid.*, 121–2.

The indefinite renewal of the NPT indicates that, despite the presence of a right of withdrawal (in Article X),[17] in one sense the grand bargain has become even stronger over the decades, although the spread of nuclear weapons to states outside the P5, to India, Pakistan, and Israel (not parties to the NPT) and North Korea (which withdrew in 2003), indicates the strain it is under.[18] The essence of the NPT is that a handful of states have the right to nuclear weapons, while others do not; but despite that inequality, the grand bargain, taken as a whole, is aimed at preserving peace and security. Furthermore, the NPT, like the CWC, has an institutional element (in the form of the IAEA), which assists in the development of the treaty by interpreting and applying its obligations (especially Article III). As Williamson states, the potential 'dual-use' capability of both nuclear materials and chemicals requires a 'high degree of intrusiveness' by the OPCW and the IAEA.[19]

2.4   Enforcement by the UN Security Council

The Security Council has also taken measures against certain states (North Korea and Iran) on the basis that their development of nuclear technology represents a threat to peace and security. The Security Council has not taken action against all states that have acquired nuclear weapons outside of the five major powers, but has focused its coercive powers on the two states that the five major powers can agree represent the greatest threat. This illustrates that it is somewhat misleading to consider that the Security Council is enforcing nonproliferation law; rather it is responding to what it agrees constitutes a threat to the peace.[20]

Following the news that North Korea had conducted an underground nuclear weapons test in October 2006, the Security Council acted under Chapter VII to condemn the test and determine that there was a

---

17 Mohamed El Baradei, the Director-General of the IAEA has argued in 2004 that the right of withdrawal should be removed from the NPT, given the importance of the treaty to international security – cited in Glennon, *supra* note 1, 132.

18 E. Louka, *Nuclear Weapons, Justice and the Law* (Cheltenham: Edward Elgar Publishing, 2011) 98–122.

19 R.L. Williamson, 'Hard Law, Soft Law, and Non-Law in Multilateral Arms Control: Some Compliance Hypotheses' (2003) 4 *Chinese Journal of International Law* 59 at 72.

20 N. Tsagourias and N.D. White, *Collective Security: Theory, Law and Practice* (Cambridge University Press, 2013) chapter 4.

threat to international peace, thereby justifying the imposition of non-forcible measures against North Korea under Article 41 of the Charter. It expressed its conviction that the non-proliferation regime embodied in the NPT should continue and that North Korea did not (and could not) have the status of an NWS under that treaty.

Since the proliferation of nuclear weapons to North Korea undermined peace, it followed that the Security Council had competence to address the nuclear test not because it was a breach of the NPT (indeed North Korea had withdrawn from the NPT), but because it was a threat to the peace. The Security Council decided that North Korea 'shall abandon all nuclear weapons and existing nuclear programmes in a complete, verifiable and irreversible manner', and 'shall act strictly in accordance with the obligations applicable to parties under the [NPT]'.[21]

In the case of Iran the security concern is that the country is developing a nuclear programme involving the enrichment of uranium that is not entirely for peaceful purposes. In Resolution 1737 of December 2006 the Security Council reaffirmed the right of NNWS states to develop nuclear energy for peaceful purposes, but expressed concern over the 'proliferation risks presented by the Iranian nuclear programme and, in this context, by Iran's continuing failure to meet the requirements of the IAEA Board of Governors and to comply with the provisions of Security Council Resolution 1696 (2006)'. Then 'mindful of its primary responsibility under the Charter of the UN for the maintenance of international peace and security' the Security Council imposed non-forcible measures under Article 41 (including targeted sanctions against nuclear scientists and others with nuclear expertise) mostly aimed at preventing Iran from acquiring the technology necessary to achieve a weapons programme, and established a Committee to oversee the implementation of those measures.

The lack of a specific finding of a threat to peace in the Resolutions on Iran is probably a result of concern in at least a section of the P5 about the use of Chapter VII language as a way of opening up Iran to unilateral military action by Israel and possibly the US, given the threats of force against Iran already issued by those countries. Indeed, at the meeting at which Resolution 1737 was adopted, the Russian

---

21   UNSC Res 1718 (2006); see more recently UNSC Res 2094 (2013) condemning a further nuclear test by North Korea and imposing further non-forcible measures under Article 41 of the UN Charter.

representative expressed his conviction that the solution to the Iranian nuclear problem would be found exclusively within the political, diplomatic and legal framework, meaning that the measures adoption in Resolution 1737 should be taken in accordance with Article 41 of the UN Charter and, therefore, involved no use of force.[22] Further, in a follow-up resolution adopted in 2010, the preamble expressly stated that 'nothing in this resolution compels States to take measures or actions exceeding the scope of this resolution, including the use of force or the threat of force'.[23]

A reluctance in the Security Council as a whole to find a threat to peace in the case of Iran's nuclear programme is still evident in Resolution 1884 (2011). This did find that the 'proliferation of weapons of mass destruction, as well as their means of delivery, continues to constitute a threat to international peace and security', but the resolution did not specifically mention Iran, although it did recall some of the Resolutions against Iran and extended the mandate of the panel of experts working with the 1737 Committee and, at the meeting at which the Resolution was adopted, it was clear that Iran was the focus of the Resolution.[24] Thus, the Security Council's measures against Iran slowly creep up the scale of measures it can adopt under Chapter VII, but have so far expressly fallen short of the threat or use of force under Article 42 of the Charter.

2.5   Biological and chemical weapons

The NPT forms part of the grand bargain or social contract as the heart of the international legal and political order, alongside the UN Charter. The BWC and the CWC, on the other hand, are 'law-making' treaties, providing a blanket prohibition upon development and possession, as well as proliferation, of their subject weapons technologies, binding upon all state parties'.[25]

Just as some domestic legislation may be seen to develop the constitution of a country, other pieces are more accurately viewed as law-making, laying down rules for all members of society, the validity of

---

22 UNSC 5612nd meeting (2006), 2.

23 UNSC Res 1929 (2010).

24 UNSC 6522nd meeting (2011).

25 Joyner, *supra* note 3, 69.

which is derived from the constitution.[26] The same analysis can be applied to the international scene, contrasting those treaties that continue the grand bargain of the UN Charter, and those that develop rules for all states. In these terms, it is argued that while the NPT is constitutional, the BWC and the CWC are law-making treaties, although all contribute to peace and security.

The NPT is 'elevated' above the other non-proliferation treaties for two reasons – the presence of the grand bargain and the fact that nuclear weapons are both the most destructive and, paradoxically, are seen as the most legitimate of the WMD – a legitimacy enhanced by the NPT itself,[27] which, unlike the other treaties, does not prohibit the WMD in question, it simply limits their proliferation. Nuclear weapons are allowed, but only in the hands of the major powers, thereby recognising the central role of both the P5 and nuclear weapons in the international order.[28]

Despite the weaknesses in the CWC and the BWC, particularly in the latter, which has no supervision machinery, Joyner confidently reports that only seven states maintain a clandestine biological weapons programme (China, Iran, Israel, Egypt, North Korea, Syria and Russia), while six have chemical weapons programmes (China, Iran, Israel, Egypt, North Korea and Syria).[29] It is noteworthy that these lists include two out of the five states at the core of the grand bargain in the UN Charter and the NPT. Clearly there remains disagreement on fairly basic issues at the heart of the grand bargain concerning the control and regulation of destructive and indiscriminate weaponry.

2.6   The UN and arms control law

WMD are subject to special agreements that, in practice, have stabilised, rather than eliminated, those weapons whose use would constitute an existential threat to peoples, states and potentially the planet. The growth in the many other types of weaponry cannot be controlled by only traditional forms of law-making, but requires greater institutional involvement.

---

26 H. Kelsen, *Pure Theory of Law* (2nd edn, University of California Press, 1967) 221–2.

27 Joyner, *supra* note 3, 67, 69.

28 See further G. Simpson, *Great Powers and Outlaw States* (Cambridge University Press, 2004) 68.

29 Joyner, *supra* note 3, 79.

The main institution in which multilateral negotiation of disarmament takes place is the Conference on Disarmament, consisting of sixty-six member states including the P5. The Conference is not formally a subsidiary body of the UN, but it has a close relationship with the UN General Assembly's First Committee, considering its reports and proposing resolutions, which are then (often) adopted by the General Assembly in its plenary sessions. In 1978 the UN General Assembly also established a Disarmament Commission, as a subsidiary body and consisting of all member states, to 'consider elements of a comprehensive programme for disarmament' and submit any recommendations thereon to the General Assembly and the Conference on Disarmament.[30]

As related in Simma, the UN system achieved notable successes in promoting the NPT in 1968, the OST in 1967, the Treaty on the Prohibition of the Emplacement of Nuclear Weapons and Other Weapons of Mass Destruction on the Sea-Bed and the Ocean Floor of 1971, the BWC of 1972 and the CWC of 1993. The Comprehensive Test Ban Treaty of 1996 is also worth mentioning although it is not yet in force.[31]

Nevertheless, 'the results actually achieved by the UN in the area of disarmament have to be regarded as somewhat meagre',[32] relying as the UN does, on recommendatory powers, which provided limited traction in the face of superpower nuclear and conventional arms rivalry during the Cold War. The UN remains largely ineffectual in the area of disarmament in the post-Cold War era of a world awash with conventional arms fuelled by a market-driven arms industry.

The proliferation in small arms and other forms of conventional weaponry has meant that the UN's goal of providing for 'human security' within states has not been fulfilled. Human security was first formulated in the UN Development Programme's (UNDP) 1994 Human Development Report, which called for individual freedom from violence and other threats to security (such as poverty and disease).[33] However, the adoption by the UN General Assembly in 2013 of an Arms Trade Treaty represents a step in the right direction. The Treaty,

---

30 K. Hailbronner and E. Klein, 'Article 11' in B. Simma (ed.), *The Charter of the United Nations: A Commentary* (2nd edn, Oxford University Press, 2002) 279; UNGA Res S-10/2 (1978).

31 Hailbronner and Klein, *supra* note 30, 279–80.

32 *Ibid.*, 280.

33 S. Chesterman and T.M. Franck, *Law and Practice of the United Nations: Documents and Commentary* (Oxford University Press, 2008) 384.

when in force, will impose a duty on state parties not to export arms (tanks, combat vehicles, artillery, combat aircraft, attack helicopters, warships, missiles, small arms) and light weapons in violation of Chapter VII obligations or with knowledge that they will be used in committing core crimes. The Treaty also imposes due diligence-type obligations on state parties requiring them to assess the likely impact of exporting arms on peace and security as well on the human rights of civilian populations.[34] Although the review mechanisms are rudimentary (consisting of a conference of the parties plus a secretariat),[35] the Arms Trade Treaty 2013 is a breakthrough in terms of finally recognising that there are limits on the sovereign rights of states as regards the acquisition of conventional armaments. This will contribute both to international peace and security and to the reduction of human suffering (as clearly stated in the purposes of the Treaty).[36]

As Keith Krause notes, the UN system has achieved some successes in diplomacy, negotiation and norm setting, but its main function in the area of arms control has been that of 'great power security governance'. Krause explains that 'no concrete action by the UN was possible until Washington and Moscow agreed in the early 1960s to move forward on arms control discussions. All major achievements – the NPT, CWC, [BWC] – required great power consensus; when it did not exist, such as in the Comprehensive Test Ban Treaty, disarmament efforts stalled'.[37]

Krause points out that the Ottawa Convention on land mines of 1997 worked around the great powers, but this was done 'deliberately and consciously outside the UN system'.[38] The same can now be said of the Cluster Weapons Convention of 2008, both treaties coming into force without a significant part of the P5 (China, Russia and the US) being on board. The trend towards negotiating and adopting major arms control treaties outside the UN system has the advantage of enabling norm setting and implementation in arms control, but it does not provide for any great power security governance.

---

34 UN Doc A/67/L.58 (2013), Arts 3, 6–7, adopted by 154 votes to 3 against (North Korea, Iran and Syria) with 23 abstentions (including China and Russia).

35 *Ibid.*, Arts 17–18.

36 *Ibid.*, Art 1.

37 K. Krause, 'Disarmament' in T.G. Weiss and S. Daws (eds), *The Oxford Handbook on the United Nations* (Oxford University Press, 2007) 297.

38 *Ibid.*

Although, the UN Security Council has taken measures against North Korea and Iran to combat the threats caused by their nuclear programmes, the UN is otherwise underdeveloped on aspects of arms control. As noted in Simma, 'the provisions of the UN Charter on disarmament and the regulation of armaments are considerably weaker that those in Art. 8 of the League of Nations Covenant, which declared that the maintenance of international peace required a reduction in armaments'.[39]

In contrast, the UN Charter provides that the General Assembly 'may consider the general principles of cooperation in the maintenance of international peace and security, including the principles governing disarmament and the regulations of armaments, and may make recommendations with regard to such principles to the Members or to the Security Council or to both'.[40] While this general recommendatory power has been used extensively by the General Assembly, the Security Council has not really upheld its part of the Charter's division of competence in disarmament. As regards the Security Council, the Charter states rather loftily that:

> in order to promote the establishment and maintenance of international peace and security with the least diversion for armaments of the world's human and economic resources, the Security Council shall be responsible for formulating, with the assistance of the Military Staff Committee referred to in Article 47, plans to be submitted to the Members of the United Nations for the establishment of a system for the regulation of armaments.[41]

While the Security Council has utilised its Chapter VII powers against specific states regarding the threat their development of WMD represents to peace, it has not developed a system for the regulation of armaments, at least in the sense of the Charter. In practice the Security Council has not fulfilled the tasks assigned to it by the UN Charter, meaning that provision has 'remained a dead letter'.[42]

The Security Council has adopted more general legislation under Chapter VII directed against WMD (in Resolution 1540 of 2004), but this really supports the non-proliferation regime established by the

---

39 Hailbronner and Klein, *supra* note 30, 278.
40 Art 11(1) UN Charter.
41 Art 26 UN Charter.
42 H-J. Schutz, 'Article 26' in Simma, *supra* note 30, 474.

NPT, BWC and the CWC, by binding states not to provide or allow any WMD capabilities to non-state actors.[43] While the treaties prevent proliferation of WMD to states, Resolution 1540 fills in a perceived gap in the regulation of WMD by requiring states not to proliferate to non-state actors, and establishes a Committee of the Security Council to oversee that obligation.[44]

2.7   Conclusion

Just as in the UN Charter there is an in-built premise in arms control law that the major powers are to be trusted with privileges in exchange for the security they can provide. The grand bargain of the NPT is premised on NWS being responsible members of international society, members who would not use these weapons unjustifiably, distinguishing them from other states unable, or deemed unable, to bear this burden. This inequality in a sense provides the basis for governance in that it distinguishes between those who wield power and those who are subject to it, and, no matter how unfair it is or appears to be, it has represented the basis of the international order since 1945.

Arms control law remains a relatively basic form of international regulation especially when considering the sophistication of many of the weapons being produced in vast quantities. This is because states generally see it as their basic right to possess the means of defending themselves, without restriction on that fundamental aspect of sovereignty. Although sovereign equality has been qualified by the NPT giving certain states the right to possess the most destructive weapons, that is something that all state parties have agreed to and, as the spread of nuclear weapons shows, has not prevented other states from acquiring nuclear weapons.

Furthermore, the major powers have not been able to secure further treaties along the lines of the NPT that recognise their military superiority by means of differential rights and duties, so that in the areas of chemical weapons, biological weapons, cluster munitions and land mines, despite the obligations therein, there is no consensus among the major powers as regards restrictions on the possession or use of these weapons. Nevertheless, even in these precarious conditions,

---

43   UNSC Res 1540 (2004).
44   See also UNSC Res 1810 (2008), UNSC Res 1977 (2011).

arms control law, no matter how flawed and rudimentary, provides the basis for developing customary as well as treaty obligations that between them will make the use of such destructive weapons unacceptable.

3 The use of force in international law

3.1 Introduction

In trying to reduce their propensity to go to war states have taken a twin-track approach by, first of all, developing a body of law directed at regulating and reducing the level of armaments held by states and, secondly, by developing a set of principles and rules regulating when states can actually use the destructive forces at their disposal.

Admittedly a heavily armed state is more likely to use force than one that is lightly armed, and an arms manufacturing state is also likely to be an arms exporting state, so that the limited progress made in arms control has impacted upon the effectiveness of any rules governing the use of force. Nonetheless, in 1945, at the end of the second global conflict of the century, states sat down and agreed a strict set of principles and rules governing the use of force in international relations.

It was no coincidence that the year in which the most devastating weapon of war was used for the first (and so far only) time against the Japanese cities of Hiroshima and Nagasaki was the same year that the UN Charter was adopted containing a clear prohibition on the use of force by states. Albert Einstein envisaged this in 1944. With the discovery of atomic energy, he said that 'everything changed' and that, therefore, 'we shall require a substantially new manner of thinking if mankind is to survive'.[1]

Prior to 1945 the *jus ad bellum* (the law regulating when force can be used) was far less developed that the *jus in bello* (the law regulating the conduct of hostilities once war had broken out) reflecting acceptance of the reality of war. Indeed, by the eighteenth century, the just war theories of Grotius and other influential jurists had fully given way

---

1 Cited in UNDP, *Human Development Report* (UN, 1994) 22.

to state practice and custom, which permitted states to wage war and engage in lesser uses of force without real legal constraint.[2]

3.2   The Covenant of the League of Nations 1919 and the Pact of Paris 1928

By the early twentieth century states had achieved a monopoly over the use of force enabling them to channel vast resources and manpower into their increasingly destructive military machines evidenced by the unimaginable levels of death and destruction of the First World War. At this stage, on the edge of self-destruction, states agreed on greater restraints on when those devastating forces could be unleashed.

The preamble to the Covenant of the League of Nations of 1919 embodied this shift, albeit incomplete, to international law and to international organisations in the regulation of the use of force. The contracting states agreed to the Covenant of the League of Nations in order to promote 'international cooperation' and 'to achieve international peace and security' by the 'acceptance of obligations not to resort to war', and by the 'firm establishment of the understandings of international law as the actual rule of conduct among Governments', and by the 'maintenance of justice and a scrupulous respect for all treaty obligations in the dealings of organised peoples with one another'.

Unfortunately, negotiations over the detail of the Covenant did not produce obligations on states, or powers conferred on the League, that matched the lofty ideals of the preamble. For instance, the obligation in Article 10, whereby member states undertook to 'respect and preserve as against external aggression the territorial integrity and existing political independence of all Members of the League', was undermined by provisions in Articles 12, 13 and 15, which permitted resort to war if stipulated peaceful settlement processes had been exhausted.[3] The League's competence was triggered by a breach of Article 10 or by a disregard by states of their obligations under Articles 12, 13, and 15.[4] Unfortunately, member states themselves were left to judge whether Articles 12, 13 and 15 had been broken before imposing sanctions, and

---

2 S.C. Neff, *War and the Law of Nations* (Cambridge University Press, 2005) 162–4.

3 Arts 12(1), 13(4), 15(6), 15(7) Covenant of the League of Nations 1919.

4 Arts 11 and 16 Covenant of the League of Nations 1919.

any military action could only be recommended by the Council acting unanimously.[5]

The League was weakened by the failure of the US to join, despite the efforts of President Woodrow Wilson in helping to craft the Covenant, and by the withdrawal of major powers such as Germany and Japan, who both pulled out in 1933, and Italy in 1937. Unlike its successor organisation, the UN, the League allowed for withdrawal upon notice,[6] illustrating that states had not yet achieved a successful transition to a constitutional system of international governance.[7] As Max Huber stated, the Covenant was 'neither contractual nor constitutional',[8] in that although it did attempt to create some form of public order in terms of laws and institutions, it allowed member states to contract out of this by following certain procedures in order to go to war and, ultimately, to withdraw from the League, thereby escaping the Covenant's obligations and undermining its pretentions towards global governance.

The defective obligations of the Covenant, which did not include a clear prohibitory norm on the use of force, appeared to have been rectified by the Treaty Providing for the Renunciation of War as an Instrument of National Policy (Pact of Paris/Kellogg Briand Pact) of 1928. Article 1 contained a declaration by the parties that they condemned 'recourse to war for the solution of international controversies', and, further, that they renounced war as an 'instrument of national policy'. Article 2 obliged the parties to settle their disputes by peaceful means.

The Pact of Paris prohibited recourse to war and had been signed up to by most of the international community, including Germany, Japan and Italy, by the outbreak of the Second World War. Although it did little to inhibit state behaviour, it did form the basis of the prosecution at Nuremberg and Tokyo of major war criminals for crimes against peace after the Second World War;[9] a breakthrough in international criminal law, and a possible deterrent for leaders planning future wars of aggression.

5   Arts 5 and 16 Covenant of the League of Nations 1919.
6   Art 1(3) of the Covenant of the League of Nations 1919.
7   A.D. McNair, 'The Function and Different Character of Treaties' (1930) 11 BYBIL 100 at 112.
8   M. Huber cited in A. Zimmern, *The League of Nations and the Rule of Law 1918–1935* (New York: Russell and Russell, 1969) 290–91.
9   See, for example, the Agreement for the Prosecution and Punishment of the Major War Criminals of the European Axis Powers (Nuremberg Charter), Art 6, 8 August 1945.

3.3   UN Charter prohibition

The Pact of Paris of 1928 represented a partial move towards a clear prohibition on the use of force. It was weakened primarily by the fact that it outlawed 'war', which had long ceased to include all 'uses of force', but its twin approach of outlawing violence and obliging states to settle their disputes by peaceful means was improved upon further by the provisions of Article 2 of the UN Charter.

While Article 2(3) of the UN Charter obliges member states to settle their disputes by peaceful means; Article 2(4) obliges all members to 'refrain in their relations from the threat or use of force against the territorial integrity or political independence of any State, or in any other manner inconsistent with the Purposes of the United Nations'.

Although there were Charter exceptions to this ban on the threat or use of force; the point is that they were clearly delimited substantive rights, not a simply series of procedural rights to wage war as in the Covenant. The exceptions in the Charter were for the right of states to individual and collective self-defence in the face of an armed attack contained in Article 51, and military measures undertaken by the UN Security Council under Article 42, in response to a threat to the peace, breach of the peace or act of aggression.

In essence the external aspect of the use of force, which hitherto had been under the monopoly of states, was brought within the framework of the UN Charter, and subject to regulation by the UN Security Council. Even the right of self-defence, historically a core sovereign right, only persisted, according to Article 51 at least, until the Security Council 'has taken measures necessary to maintain international peace and security'. Nevertheless, the monopoly on the external use of force that states hitherto enjoyed was only formally subjected to the UN Charter, there being no transference of military capability to the UN, which, as we shall see in Chapter 5, weakens the effectiveness of the post-1945 collective security system.

Nonetheless, unlike the Covenant, the Charter separated the prohibition on the use of force from the effectiveness of the collective machinery for keeping the peace, by placing military action by the Security Council as an exception to a ban on the use of force rather than a condition for its application. Furthermore, the right of self-defence was only restricted by the UN Charter if the Security Council took necessary measures; although it remained restricted by the conditions inherent in the right; such as proportionality, immediacy and necessity.

In its first contentious case concerning a dispute that had arisen between Albania and the UK in the Corfu Channel, in 1946, the International Court of Justice (ICJ) confirmed that the rule prohibiting the use of force was independent from the effectiveness or otherwise of the collective security machinery set up by the Charter.[10] In response to loss of life and damage caused by mines to two of its naval ships when passing through the Corfu Channel, the UK sent a larger naval operation through the Channel to clear mines from Albanian territorial waters in order to secure evidence of Albanian wrongdoing, further arguing that such an operation did not result in any loss of territory or political independence by Albania.

That this was an early challenge to the Charter rules on the use of force was clear. The UK, used to exerting its power by military means in the past, including the use of gunboat diplomacy, and dissatisfied with the lack of any international means of impugning Albania, was intent on securing compelling evidence of mine-laying in international straits as well as teaching Albania a lesson, arguing that such limited uses or threats of force did not violate any rules prohibiting force.[11]

While finding Albania did bear responsibility for the presence of mines in its waters,[12] the Court dismissed the actions and arguments of the UK in no uncertain terms, as a failed attempt to resurrect a right of forceful intervention which had 'in the past given rise to the most serious abuses and as such cannot, whatever be the defects in international organization, find a place in international law'. The argument of self-protection or self-help, put forward by the UK government, was also dismissed in clear terms: 'between independent States, respect for territorial sovereignty is an essential foundation of international relations' and, therefore, 'to ensure respect for international law' the Court declared that the 'action of the British navy constituted a violation of Albanian sovereignty'.[13]

---

10 *Corfu Channel Case (Merits)*, 1949 ICJ Rep 4.
11 I. Brownlie, *International Law and the Use of Force by States* (Oxford University Press, 1963) 266.
12 *Corfu Channel Case*, *supra* note 10, 17–22.
13 *Ibid.*, 35.

Of course, the fact that the prohibition on the use of force was so strongly reaffirmed in 1946 was not unexpected given that the norm had just been agreed; the more important question is whether such a rule, and the consensus behind it, could survive the Cold War, when the superpowers seem to disregard it at will; and, if still intact by 1989, could it then adapt to and survive the post-Cold War spread of asymmetrical warfare and violence by states and non-state actors? It is not surprising that the demise of the norm has often been declared in the literature (most famously by Thomas Franck in 1970[14]), but it is not so easy to kill a fundamental norm that has taken centuries of warfare, death and destruction to formulate and adopt.

3.4   The prohibition as a paper rule?

An examination of state practice, in the form of what states do, may suggest that the prohibition on the use of force is in fact a mere paper rule that is regularly breached.[15] To put it another way, although there is a treaty rule that prohibits the threat or use of force in international relations subject to certain limited exceptions, customary practice seems to reject the normative validity of Article 2(4), instead it manifests a belief in a different set of rules or, indeed, a condition of no regulation of the use of force.

However, this essentially behaviourist stance ignores how law not only has an external aspect in the form of behaviour but also an internal aspect. Borrowing from Hart,[16] an alien observing planet Earth from afar would see threatening behaviour and outbreaks of kinetic violence between states and might well conclude that violence was endemic, but this would ignore the vast majority of peaceful states and the normal condition of peaceful relations between them, as well as the reactions of the majority of states to violations of the peace by a handful of violent states.

Customary law has both an internal and an external aspect. Customary law is what states do while accepting that they are under a duty or

---

14 See, for example, T.M. Franck, 'Who Killed Article 2(4)? Or: Changing Norms Governing the Use of Force by States' (1970) 64 *AJIL* 809.

15 I.I. Dore, *International Law and the Superpowers: Normative Order in a Divided World* (New Brunswick: Rutgers University Press, 1984).

16 H.L.A. Hart, *The Concept of Law* (Oxford: Clarendon, 1961) 87–8.

have a right to do so (*opinio juris sive necessitates*).[17] *Opinio juris* is best understood in terms of the internalisation of a norm by a state, so that when it is asserting its rights or following its duties in relation to other states, its agents will make declarations to that effect; or when other states are not acting in accordance with their obligations it will condemn those states for breach. *Opinio juris* is an essential element of customary law and is the element that explains the continued validity of the norm prohibiting the use of force as a rule of custom. In treaty law there is a parallel principle – *pacta sunt servanda* – which explains the obligatory force of treaties.[18]

That this remains so, even in the face of clear violations of the norm, is best illustrated by an example from the Cold War, when the superpowers seemed to use force whenever their spheres of influence were under threat. In 1979, the Soviet Union invaded Afghanistan but claimed that the Afghan government had requested Soviet intervention pursuant to a treaty of friendship between the two states, to protect it from external intervention. The argument was, in essence, one of collective self-defence, the Soviet Union arguing that it had been requested to send troops to protect Afghanistan from being a victim of a breach of Article 2(4).[19]

The argument was clearly spurious since the request for assistance came from the very regime that the Soviet troops had just installed, but it illustrates that even though the Soviet Union was prepared to use force for regime change it was not prepared to say it had the right to do so. Furthermore, the Soviet actions were roundly and regularly condemned by the rest of the world in the form of General Assembly resolutions, which were adopted annually until Soviet withdrawal from Afghanistan in 1989.[20]

This very important point was emphasised in 1986 in the *Nicaragua* case, when the ICJ in effect confronted the argument that state practice was not in conformity with the prohibition of the use of force.

---

17 Art 38(1)(b) Statute of the International Court of Justice 1945: 'general practice accepted as law'.
18 Art 26 Vienna Convention on the Law of Treaties 1969: 'Every treaty is binding upon the parties to it and must be performed by them in good faith'.
19 UNSC 2190th meeting (1980).
20 Starting with UNGA Res ES-6 (1980).

The Court does not consider that, for a rule to be established as customary, the corresponding practice must be in absolute rigorous conformity
with the rule. In order to deduce the existence of customary rules, the
Court deems it sufficient that the conduct of States should, in general, be
consistent with such rules, and that instances of State conduct inconsistent with a given rule should generally have been treated as breaches of
that rule, not as indications of the recognition of a new rule. If a State
acts in a way *prima facie* incompatible with a recognised rule, but defends
its conduct by appealing to exceptions or justifications contained within
the rule itself, then whether or not the State's conduct is in fact justifiable
on that basis, the significance of that attitude is to confirm rather than
weaken the rule.[21]

Indeed, the prohibition of the use of force is not only a rule of custom
but is recognised as a peremptory rule of international law (*jus cogens*)
from which no derogation is allowed.[22] *Jus cogens* are the most fundamental norms of international law. The prohibition of violence except
in clear self-defence or under the authority of a central body is perhaps
the most important hallmark of any society, but, moreover, underpins
any legal order. In a sense, the prohibition on the use of force can
withstand many violations simply because without it any attempt to
construct an international legal order would be doomed to failure.
However, there must come a point when violence is so widespread and
appears to be spiralling out of control, that the validity of the whole
legal order is in question.[23]

Given that we have not reached such levels of self-destruction, it follows that the prohibition on the use of force remains the most fundamental norm in international law. However, it is entirely possible that
further exceptions to the prohibition might be carved out particularly
as values change. As shall be seen in Chapter 7, there has been a shift
in the international consensus from a central concern with state security towards human security,[24] so that the prohibition on existential
threats and attacks on peoples and groups is not only recognised as *jus
cogens* but enforcement measures, including military action taken to
prevent such egregious violations, are permissible, arguably obligatory,

---

21 *Case Concerning Military and Paramilitary Activities in and Against Nicaragua (Nicaragua v
United States)*, 1986 ICJ Rep, 14 at 98.

22 A. Orakhelashvili, *Peremptory Norms under International Law* (Oxford University Press, 2006)
50–51.

23 H. Kelsen, *Principles of International Law* (New York: Rinehart and Winston, 1967) 551–88.

24 Introduced in UNDP, *Human Development Report, supra* note 1, 22.

even though not one of the treaty exceptions to the prohibition on the use of force.[25] This crucial issue will be returned to in Chapters 5 and 8 when considering the argument that states have the right of humanitarian intervention and, further, by the development of the idea of the responsibility to protect in the face of genocide, crimes against humanity and systematic war crimes.

3.5   Political doctrines

Unfortunately international law is not as neat and tidy as the above analysis suggests. Further consideration reveals that many reasons and justifications are given for military interventions; so that the issue becomes as to whether it is possible to distinguish arguments of law and *opinio juris* from arguments of policy and self-interest.

Interventions within major powers' respective spheres have often been accompanied by the statement of a 'doctrine', outlining a policy of the circumstances in which force will be used, traceable to the Monroe Doctrine of 1823 by which the US warned European states to refrain from further interventions in the Americas. These doctrines appear to fly in the face of Article 2(4). It is interesting to note that the Monroe Doctrine was recognised in the League of Nations Covenant in 1919,[26] further undermining that treaty's move towards international law as a basis of settling disputes.

The Johnson Doctrine, for example, was an attempt to justify armed intervention by the US in the Dominican Republic in 1965, when that country was in a state of civil war. President Johnson justified the intervention on the basis that 'the American nation cannot permit the establishment of another Communist dictatorship in the Western Hemisphere'.[27]

There was a parallel Soviet doctrine – the Brezhnev Doctrine – enunciated in 1968 to justify politically the Soviet Union's armed intervention in Czechoslovakia to overthrow the government of Alexander Dubcek. Brezhnev spoke in terms of when 'internal and external forces hostile

---

25 N. Tsagourias and N.D. White, *Collective Security: Law, Theory and Practice* (Cambridge University Press, 2013) chapters 3 and 4.

26 Art 21 Covenant of the League of Nations 1919.

27 (1965) 52 US Dept. of State Bulletin 745.

to socialism' diverted a socialist state away from socialism towards capitalism it became 'no longer merely a problem for the country's people, but a common problem, the concern of all socialist countries', which necessitated the 'extraordinary measure' of 'military assistance' to the beleaguered state.[28]

To an extent these doctrines can be seen as 'political', not ones that subvert the basic legal rule prohibiting force.[29] The superpowers always made sure that there was a separate explanation, couched in legal language and based on recognised or claimed rights, for their interventions. In the case of the Dominican Republic, the US argued that it had the right to protect its nationals in addition to the authority of a regional organisation (the Organisation of American States (OAS)) for its actions;[30] while in the instance of Czechoslovakia, the USSR made its usual cynical argument of self-defence.[31]

In this way, such doctrines recognised the separation of politics from international law, and an assertion that, in the particular instance, politics were more important than law. This reality is neatly encapsulated by Dean Acheson's statement after the Cuban Missile Crisis of 1962, when the brinkmanship between the US and USSR was at its keenest, with the Soviet Union intent on supplying nuclear missiles to Cuba and the US intent on blocking such supplies by means of a quarantine placed around Cuba.

> I must conclude that the propriety of the Cuban quarantine . . . is not a legal issue. The power, position and prestige of the United States had been challenged by another state; and law does not deal with such questions of ultimate power – power that comes close to the sources of sovereignty.[32]

In contrast, the Bush Doctrine formulated in September 2002 took the form of a direct challenge to the international legal order, for it represented an attempt to change the law rather than a recognition that law and power may diverge. Following from the terrorist attacks by al-Qaeda on the US of 11 September 2001 the Doctrine focused on the threat posed by 'terrorist organizations of global reach and any

---

28 (1968) 20 Current Digest of the Soviet Press, no. 46, 3–4.

29 *Nicaragua* case, *supra* note 21, at para 207.

30 UNSC 1196th meeting, (1965).

31 UNSC 1141st meeting (1968).

32 D. Acheson. 'Response to Panel: The Cuban Quarantine – Implications for the Future' (1963) 14 ASIL *Proceedings* 14–15.

terrorist or state sponsor of terrorism, which attempts to gain or use weapons of mass destruction'. Under the Doctrine the US claimed to be able to 'exercise our right of self-defence by acting preemptively against . . . terrorists, to prevent them from doing harm against our people and our country'; further, 'to stop rogue states and their terrorist clients before they are able to threaten or use weapons of mass destruction against the US and [its] allies'.[33]

Despite the worrying claim of a right of pre-emptive self-defence that is so wide as to be virtually unregulated by international law, the Bush Doctrine should be seen not as a statement of international law, but as an attempt to change international law, which states can accept or reject; and, at least, there is little evidence of states positively accepting such a radical change.

Despite this, the US continues to practice a policy of targeted uses of force against suspected terrorists, relying largely on acquiescence and the inability of the rest of the world to stop it; and this is oft-couched in the language of self-defence. For example Attorney General Holder justified the killing of Osama bin Laden by US special forces in Pakistan in May 2011 as an act of national self-defence.[34]

3.6   Self-defence

One of the most sacred trusts placed in the government of any state by its people is to defend that country from its enemies. The classical jurist Emmerich de Vattel declared in 1758 that '[s]elf-defense against an unjust attack is not only a right which every Nation has, but it is a duty, and one of its most sacred duties'.[35]

As states have been the subjects of international law since before the seventeenth century, the rights and duties recognised in customary international law have included the right to defend the nation if attacked.[36] Indeed, the notion of self-defence transcends law and legal

---

33   See http://www.state.gov/documents/organization/63562.pdf.

34   'Bin Laden death not assassination – Eric Holder' (*BBC News*, 12 May 2011) at http://www.bbc.co.uk/news/world-us-canada-13370919.

35   E. de Vattel, *The Law of Nations, or the Principles of Natural Law, Applied to the Conduct and to the Affairs of Nations and of Sovereigns* (translated by T. Nugent, Indianapolis: Liberty, 2008) 246.

36   V. Lowe, *International Law* (Oxford University Press, 2007) 8–10. See generally D. Kritsiotis, 'A Study of the Scope and Operation of the Rights of Individual and Collective Self-Defence under

systems, in that it is not possible to imagine a legal order that did not allow the subjects of that order to defend themselves from attack.[37]

In the minimal conditions of a legal order, what Hart identified as the *'minimum content* of Natural Law',[38] embodied in the international legal order in the concept of *jus cogens*, there are basic laws protecting persons (states) and property (territory), which are fundamental for the survival of that legal order as well as the actors within it. No matter how centralised the use of force becomes, no police force will be able to supplant the right to defend oneself from attack. In this sense, self-defence is a 'natural' or 'inherent' right.

The modern international law of self-defence could be said to have finally emerged once there was a clear prohibition on the use of force, and that only occurred with the UN Charter in 1945. Given that self-defence is a right to respond to an unlawful attack against a person or state, or in other words, a victim's response to an attacker's breach of a legal duty not to attack,[39] self-defence as a precisely defined legal right will depend on there being a clear prohibition on using force in the international legal order.[40]

A certain amount of controversy surrounds the embodiment of the right of self-defence in the UN Charter, which, in Article 51, is quite narrow in its preservation of the 'inherent right of individual or collective self-defence if an armed attack occurs against a Member of the United Nations'. In particular, it is often stated that Article 51 does not fully encapsulate the pre-existing inherent right of self-defence, which, it is argued, is wider, particularly when anticipating an armed attack.[41]

While the classic formulation of the right, located in diplomatic correspondence between the US and the UK concerning an anticipatory strike by the British on the ship *The Caroline* in 1837, does suggest

International Law' in N.D. White and C. Henderson (eds), *Research Handbook on International Conflict and Security Law* (Cheltenham: Edward Elgar Publishing, 2013) 170.

37 N.D. White, 'Review Essay: Defending Humanity' (2009) 10 *MJIL* 379-93.

38 Hart, *supra* note 16 (emphasis in original).

39 D. Rodin, *War and Self-Defense* (Oxford University Press, 2002) 29–30.

40 Y. Dinstein, *War, Aggression and Self-Defence* (Cambridge University Press, 2005) 178.

41 D.W. Bowett, *Self-Defence in International Law* (Manchester University Press, 1958) 187; M.S. McDougal and F. Feliciano, *Law and Minimum World Public Order* (Yale University Press, 1961) 232–41.

that some degree of anticipation of an armed attack is allowed, it still conveys the need for imminence, in other words that the attack is occurring or about to occur. The phrase used in *The Caroline* was that the state exercising the right of self-defence has to 'show a necessity of self-defence, instant, overwhelming, leaving no choice of means and no moment for deliberation'.[42]

The text of Article 51 can be read narrowly to require a state to wait for an attack to occur in the form of tanks or missiles, for example, crossing its frontier. However, at such a point, the first blow has been landed and normally a right of self-defence entitles the defender to anticipate that blow and take defensive measures, not simply by preparing its defences but by parrying that blow before it lands and landing one of its own if that is necessary and proportionate. Fine judgements have to be made by the attacked state so as to tread the line between a 'pre-emptive strike against a feared aggressor' which is 'illegal force used too soon', and 'retaliation against a successful aggressor' which is 'illegal force used too late'.[43]

Translating these parameters on to the international stage sometimes appears difficult: for example, it appeared that the UK's response to the Argentinian invasion of the Falklands in 1982 was too slow as it took several weeks for the British task force to be assembled and then sail to the islands, where British forces forcefully ejected the occupiers. However, in the context of the movement of huge military resources hundreds of miles, the UK's response was a legitimate act of continuous and unbroken self-defence and not a punitive reprisal against Argentina for a breach of international law. Punitive reprisals, though accepted in classical international law as a means of enforcing the law,[44] did not survive the outlawing of the use of force in the UN Charter.[45]

---

42 *The Caroline (Exchange of Diplomatic Notes between the United Kingdom . . . and the United States)*, Letter from Mr Webster to Mr Fox (24 April 1841), (1842) British and Foreign State Papers 1129, 1138.

43 G. Fletcher, *Basic Concepts of Criminal Law* (Oxford University Press, 1998) 133; Rodin, *supra* note 39, 41.

44 *Naulilaa Case* (1928) 2 RIAA 1012.

45 Declaration on Principles of International Law Concerning Friendly Relations and Co-operation Among States in Accordance with the Charter of the United Nations, UNGA Res 2625 (1970), which states, inter alia, that 'States have a duty to refrain from acts of reprisal involving the use of force'.

Anticipating an armed attack is also hugely problematic for states. Faced with, amongst other pieces of evidence, what appeared to be the mobilisation of Egyptian forces, belligerent statements by President Nasser of Egypt, and the pulling out of the UN peacekeeping force as a result of the withdrawal of Egyptian consent to its presence on its territory, Israel struck the first devastating blow against Egypt in the Six Day War of 1967. However, was there sufficient evidence of an imminent armed attack against Israel? The answer to this question is found in the 'correct definition of imminence',[46] which lies between waiting for the tanks or missiles to cross the border (which is too late for the attacked state), and striking first in the face of what *might be* preparations to attack (which is force used pre-emptively). If pre-emptive force is permitted, this would grant states with the military capability a 'licence to attack every strategic enemy'.[47]

Self-defence has to be interpreted in the light of changing conditions, especially changes in the nature of the threat and the development of new weapons. The era of nuclear weapons and other WMD and, more recently, of the suicide bomber, have presented challenges to international law and the way states interpret the right of self-defence.

It was argued that the acquisition of nuclear missiles by Cuba in 1962 entitled the US to impose a quarantine around Cuba as a forceful response in self-defence.[48] However, there was no evidence of an imminent attack against the US about to come from Cuba. If anything, Cuba could have made a stronger case that it was about to be attacked by the US, given the CIA-backed attempted Bay of Pigs invasion of Cuba in 1961.

This usefully highlights the weakness of a claimed right to pre-emptive defence, since both sides in a spiralling arms race, particularly one involving WMD (India and Pakistan for example), justifiably see the other state as a threat and, therefore, both would conceivably have a co-existing right to (pre-emptive) self-defence. A situation where both states using force against each other are exercising the right of self-defence would clearly be incompatible with any international legal order.

---

46 G.P. Fletcher and J.D. Ohlin, *Defending Humanity: When Force is Justified and Why* (Oxford University Press, 2008) 156.

47 *Ibid.*

48 M.S. McDougal, 'The Soviet-Cuban Quarantine and Self-Defense' (1963) 57 *AJIL* 597 at 602–3.

3.7   Modern threats and self-defence

The above analysis still leaves the problem of how states can respond to nuclear threats, as well as threats of attacks by missiles with conventional warheads, given the danger of states being sitting targets if they wait for the attack to materialise.[49] We return to the idea of imminence and put it into the context of highly destructive weapons, where it would indeed be far too late to wait for the armed attack to cross the frontiers of a state. Indeed, in many instances, it would be too late to wait until the attack has been launched from the aggressor state. It would also depend on the technology of the defending state, so that if it had an effective missile shield it could still defend itself after an attack has been launched, but a state without such technology could well argue that it had the right to strike as soon as it detected that a launch sequence had been initiated by the aggressor state.

Advances in technology have led to attacks that are not directly kinetic – primarily cyber-attacks on another state's computer system, although their effects may cause damage, as with the Stuxnet attack on Iran's nuclear plants in 2010. This attack resulted in the destruction of Iranian centrifuges, essential for the enrichment of uranium. Such attacks can, exceptionally, amount to a use of force, even an armed attack, justifying the exercise of the right of self-defence if they cause damage and have scale and effects.[50]

The law of self-defence is still adapting to the increasingly destructive acts of non-state actors, particularly terrorist organisations of global reach such as al-Qaeda. Despite an ambiguous statement by the ICJ that self-defence is confined to attacks by one state against another state,[51] Article 51 does not confine self-defence to attacks by states and it would make no sense for a state that is being attacked by a foreign non-state actor not to be able to claim the right of self-defence, calling upon its allies, if necessary, to help protect itself.

---

49 The International Court of Justice did not help to resolve this dilemma in its advisory opinion on the *Legality of the Threat or Use of Nuclear Weapons*, (1996) ICJ Rep 226.

50 For discussion see R. Buchan, 'Cyber Attacks: Unlawful Use of Force or Prohibited Intervention?' (2012) 17 *JCSL* 211; N. Tsagourias, 'Cyber Attacks, Self-Defence and the Problem of Attribution' (2012) 17 *JCSL* 229.

51 *Legal Consequences of the Construction of a Wall in the Occupied Palestinian Territories*, (2004) ICJ Rep 136, paras 138–41.

The UN Security Council appeared to endorse a right of right of self-defence in response to terrorist attacks, when it recognised such in condemning the attack on the US by al-Qaeda operatives using hijacked airliners as weapons on 11 September 2001; an attack which resulted in the loss of nearly 3,000 lives and the destruction of the World Trade Center.[52]

Of course, the moment for defending itself against the 9/11 attack had passed so that when the US (and the UK) reacted by using force against Afghanistan (where al-Qaeda was based) in October 2001, it appeared to be force used too late (a reprisal). However, the argument was that further terrorist attacks were being planned from Afghanistan requiring anticipatory action by the US and its allies and, further, that these attacks were imminent, and therefore force was not being used too soon.[53] This would justify the proportionate use of force against al-Qaeda bases in Afghanistan, but the additional use of force against the de facto government of Afghanistan (the Taliban) is more problematic.

The problem is that once a state uses force in an anticipatory way to forestall imminent terrorist attacks it will have to use force in another state's territory where the terrorists are based (the host state). The fact that the host state has allowed or harboured the terrorists does not mean that it too is an aggressor against the target state.

In the *Nicaragua* case of 1986, brought by Nicaragua against the US, inter alia, for its support of the Contra insurgency against the Nicaraguan government, the ICJ relied on the General Assembly's 1974 Definition of Aggression[54] as to when a state, by supporting an armed group in another state, can be said to have committed an armed attack against that state.

Article 3(g) of the Definition of Aggression states that an act of aggression is committed by a state by the 'sending . . . of armed bands, groups, irregulars or mercenaries, which carry out acts of armed force against another State of such gravity as to amount to the acts listed above', which include invasion, attack, and bombardment, 'or its substantial

---

52 UNSC Res 1368 (2001).
53 The US and UK claimed the action in Afghanistan was an exercise of the right of anticipatory self-defence (see UN Doc S/2001/946 and UN Doc S/2001/947).
54 UNGA Res 3314 (1974).

involvement therein'. The Court, having found this provision to represent customary international law, went on to state:

> The Court sees no reason to deny that, in customary law, the prohibition of armed attacks may apply to the sending by a State of armed bands to the territory of another State, if such an operation, because of its scale and effects, would have been classified as an armed attack rather than as a mere frontier incident had it been carried out by regular armed forces. But the Court does not believe that the concept of 'armed attack' includes not only acts by armed bands where such acts occur on a significant scale but also assistance to rebels in the form of the provision of weapons or logistical or other support. Such assistance may be regarded as a threat or use of force, or amount to intervention in the internal or external affairs of other States.[55]

By this reasoning the Court made it clear that self-defence is only triggered by an armed attack, and not by a threat or use of force, or other form of intervention; and that the support by Nicaragua for the FMLN rebels in El Salvador (by supplying them with arms) did not amount to an armed attack justifying the counter-intervention in Nicaragua by the US as a form of collective self-defence of El Salvador.[56] This reasoning does not render the state where the insurgency is occurring defenceless. Such a state has no general legal restrictions on its right to acquire weaponry and, indeed, there is state practice that would allow it to call upon its allies to help it take forceful action against the insurgents.[57]

Thus, it is only if the host state sends terrorists or 'is substantially involved therein' that it can be deemed to have committed an armed attack, justifying self-defence by the attacked states and its allies. If the host state's involvement with a terrorist group on its territory falls short of this, then although it will have committed a breach of international law by allowing its territory to be used for launching attacks, it has not committed an attack itself. This would normally mean that any defensive action taken against the terrorists should not be directed at the government of the host state so as to undermine its political independence, although it has been argued that a state acting in self-defence extra-territorially against terrorists may have to use

---

55 *Nicaragua* case, *supra* note 21, at para 195.
56 *Ibid.*, paras 160, 211, 230.
57 *Ibid.*, paras 210, 246.

force against the host state's government if that is necessary to defend itself.[58]

If a host state is unable or unwilling to tackle a terrorist organisation operating from its territory then, arguably, it temporarily loses some of its sovereign rights over territory in the face of a targeted and proportionate use of force by a state faced with an imminent attack by that organisation. It does not mean that the host state is more broadly a legitimate target of a defensive response,[59] unless it comes to the aid of the terrorist organisation.

When a state, such as Israel, is subject to constant, relatively minor terrorist attacks against it, it is entitled to defend itself from those attacks and take action to forestall imminent attacks. It is not entitled to defend itself by massive 'cleansing' operations such as those launched against Hezbollah in Lebanon in 2006 and Hamas in Gaza in 2009. To accept Israel's argument that an 'accumulation of events' entitles it to pick and choose when to launch its counter-terrorist military operations would, in effect, allow states to elevate low level uses of force that occur over a period of time into the equivalent of one massive attack, when the reality is that the 'pin-prick' attacks remain as such and should be defended against accordingly.[60]

3.8   Conclusion

The Charter rules on the use of force are designed, and have been further developed (by the ICJ and by various UN resolutions), to prevent the escalation of conflict. The rules do this by permitting a state only to exercise its right of self-defence (either individually or collectively in concert with its allies), in response to an armed attack against it.

If faced with a threat of force (that has not yet amounted to an imminent attack), or a use of force of lesser gravity or scale and effects than an armed attack (for example a minor frontier incident, or an insurgency supported but not sent by an outside state), the victim state does

---

58 E. Wilmshurst 'The Chatham House Principles of International Law on the Use of Force in Self-Defence', (2006) 55 *ICLQ* 963, principle 6.

59 *Case Concerning Armed Activities on the Territory of the Congo (Democratic Republic of the Congo v Uganda)*, (2005) ICJ Rep 168 at paras 146–7.

60 A similar US argument was dismissed (on the facts) by the ICJ in *Case Concerning Oil Platforms (Islamic Republic of Iran v United States of America)*, (2003) ICJ Rep 161 at para 64.

not have the right of self-defence against the state making the threats or supporting the insurgency.

But this does not leave the victim state defenceless. In the face of a threat of force against it, such a state can, indeed should, prepare itself (along with its allies) to deter and, if necessary, parry any imminent attack. If faced with an insurgency being fuelled against it, a state can take forceful measures against the insurgents and can call on its allies to help with arming, training, and (more controversially) fighting the insurgency.

Without these rules, which admittedly are not always obeyed by states, there is a greater danger that conflict would become endemic in an anarchic world of remorseless blows and counter-blows,[61] of intervention and counter-intervention, which could finish with a third, and potentially existential, world war.

---

61 T.J. Farer, 'Beyond the Charter Frame: Unilateralism or Condominium?' (2002) 96 *AJIL* 359.

4   The regulation of private violence

4.1   The emergence of Private Military and Security Companies (PMSCs)

The late twentieth century witnessed a significant growth of private companies providing a range of military and security services, both within their national states and abroad. Such PMSCs are potentially a resource that might be deployed for the purposes of peace and security, but because private security might lead to a weakening of states' monopoly on the use of force this could, alternatively, result in greater uncontrolled violence in the world. Ballard argues that it is 'no coincidence that, as the claim to the monopoly of legitimate violence increasingly becomes privatized, one sees the decline of the modern state'.[1]

The growth in outsourcing of military and security functions has been the most extensive within two of the P5 (the US and the UK), where it is seen as almost inevitable in the political and economic conditions of the twenty-first century. In the UK the view was taken that the end of the Cold War produced a 'peace dividend' in the form of much reduced military establishments, since massive standing military capability built up to try and match an anticipated Soviet onslaught across the North German plains was no longer necessary. Instead, what was needed was a smaller mobile military able to carry out core combat and peace-enforcement functions in trouble spots around the world, with other military and security functions being purchased as and when necessary.[2]

---

1 K.M. Ballard, 'The Privatization of Military Affairs: An Historical Look into the Evolution of Private Military History' in T. Jager and G. Kummel (eds), *Private Military and Security Companies: Chances, Problems, Pitfalls and Prospects* (Wiesbaden: Verlag, 2007) 37 at 41.

2 A. Bohm, K. Senior and A. White, 'The UK: National Self-Regulation and International Norms' in C. Bakker and M. Sossai (eds), *Multilevel Regulation of Military and Security Contractors: The Interplay Between International, European and Domestic Norms* (Oxford: Hart, 2012) 309.

While the end of the arms race between the superpowers (and their allies) is an important explanation for the growth of PMSCs, there are a number of other factors that help to explain the emergence of PMSCs with global reach, not only within the US and the UK, but also in other countries, including the other three permanent members of the Security Council – Russia, France and, to a lesser extent, China. Firstly, the end of the Cold War helped to entrench a dominant ideology of free markets and privatization, with a commensurate decline in the role of government, which inevitably erodes even core state functions such as security. Secondly, the pool of ex-servicemen created by the peace dividend, consisting of highly trained relatively young professional soldiers who were not satisfied with taking a job as security guards outside nightclubs, provide a ready supply of personnel for PMSCs. Thirdly, the use of PMSCs by governments is not subject to the same level of democratic review as the regular forces: the body count is of British or American soldiers killed in Afghanistan or Iraq, and not contractors working for PMSCs. Finally, governments contracting with PMSCs are certainly putting some distance between themselves and the acts and omissions of the PMSCs and therefore there might be an expectation that governments are contracting out responsibility when things go wrong, an issue which goes to the very heart of the regulation of private violence by means of international law and one that will be returned to in this chapter.[3]

4.2   Forms of responsibility for private violence

Some examples drawn from Iraq during the occupation and subsequent military enforcement action by the US and the UK after the invasion of 2003 will serve to illustrate the differences in practice in terms of both apportioning responsibility and in the forms of accountability for wrongful acts committed there by regular soldiers and by security contractors. There has been no general recognition by the US or the UK that they bore responsibility as states for internationally wrongful acts committed by their troops in Iraq. Nonetheless, the case of Baha Mousa illustrates that when soldiers commit serious violations of international law (in that case unlawfully torturing and then taking the life of an Iraqi civilian while in a British detention centre

---

3 See generally C. Lehnardt, 'Private Military Companies' in N.D. White and C. Henderson (eds), *Research Handbook on International Conflict and Security Law* (Cheltenham: Edward Elgar Publishing, 2013) 421.

in Basra), the soldiers themselves may be held criminally responsible under national and international law (as evidenced by the conviction of Corporal Payne by a British court martial);[4] liability that might be extended to other members of the armed forces following the Public Inquiry of Sir William Gage.[5] In addition to individual responsibility, the state bore responsibility for the actions of its agents (as determined by the European Court of Human Rights (ECtHR) in a case brought against the UK[6]), and as evidenced by the payment by the UK of compensation to the family of the deceased.[7]

While abuse of prisoners by the definitive state agent – the regular soldier – can lead to both state and individual responsibility; there is a great deal less certainty as regards equivalent actions by private contractors. Iraqi prisoners held by the US at Abu Ghraib prison in Baghdad were abused by both US soldiers and private contractors whose companies (Titan and CACI) provided translation and interrogation services. There followed the criminal conviction of a number of US soldiers, including Lynndie England and Charles Graner, but no criminal cases were brought against Titan or CACI contractors, even though a number had been identified by US army investigators as being culpable of prisoner abuse. Furthermore, there was a failed class action brought by Iraqi victims and their families before US courts.[8] Thus, neither state, nor individual responsibility, nor, indeed, corporate responsibility was engaged in this instance when prisoner abuse was undertaken by contractors.

The point is not that state and individual responsibility automatically follows when soldiers commit abuse, while no such responsibility follows when the same acts are committed under government contract with private security personnel. States are reluctant to own up in both instances. Furthermore, courts martial can struggle to deliver justice in relation to crime scenes thousands of miles away and in the face of 'regimental amnesia', whereby comrades-in-arms are unwilling to

---

4 G. Simpson, 'The Death of Baha Mousa' (2007) 8 *MJIL* 340.

5 Sir William Gage, 'The Report of the Baha Mousa Inquiry', 8 September 2011, at http://www.bahamousainquiry.org/report/index.htm.

6 *Al-Skeini v United Kingdom* (Application No. 55721/07) ECtHR, 7 July 2011.

7 M. Weaver and R. Norton-Taylor, 'MoD to Pay £3m to Iraqis Tortured by British Troops', *The Guardian*, 10 July 2008.

8 *Saleh v Titan Corp and CACI International*, US Court of Appeals for DC, 11 September 2009 (No. 08-7008) available at http://www.asser.nl/upload/documents/DomCLIC/Docs/NLP/US/Saleh_Court_of_Appeals_11-09-2009.pdf.

testify against one of their own. The point is that state and individual
responsibility are accepted in principle for acts of state agents, while
they are not, at least not without additional conditions, in the case of
private contractors.

4.3   States and violence

An historical examination of the use of force by states shows that
after the Peace of Westphalia 1648 states strove to monopolise violence internally – over lawless territories or groups, or those wanting
to 'opt out' of the state by secession, or otherwise not recognising
the authority of the sovereign.[9] However, in the case of external violence against enemy sovereigns, force was not fully nationalised until
the period from the mid-nineteenth century to the early twentieth
century. Before that, armies were largely composed of a mixture
of regular soldiers and hired mercenaries; navies were a mixture of
state warships and privateers; and, moreover, colonisation was often
undertaken not by sovereign forces, but by companies chartered by
governments.[10]

The two world wars of the twentieth century were fought by citizen
armies, the state being able to marshal all its resources in this way;
but corporate involvement was still present. The US would not have
been able to move from peace to war so quickly in 1941, following
the Japanese attack against Pearl Harbor, if it had not been for private
companies fulfilling many military services and functions apart from
combat.[11]

By the mid-twentieth century international law had developed sufficiently to restrict the external use of force by states, culminating
in the UN Charter, which attempted to centralise authority over the
use of force in the Security Council. After 1945, international law was
further developed to challenge the state's internal monopoly on violence, especially when it descends to the level of egregious violations
of human security amounting to genocide, crimes against humanity or

---

9 E. Krahmann, 'Private Security Companies and the State Monopoly on Violence: A Case of Norm
   Change?' (2009) 88 PRIF-Reports 2.

10 J.E. Thomson, *Mercenaries, Pirates and Sovereigns* (Princeton University Press, 1994) 22–35.

11 M. Likosky, 'The Privatization of Violence' in S. Chesterman and A. Fisher (eds), *Private Security,
   Public Order: The Outsourcing of Public Services and Its Limits* (Oxford University Press, 2009) 11
   at 15–16.

widespread war crimes. The impact of modern outsourcing on these state-based laws and structures has to be considered after first looking at the historical precedents.

4.4   The British East India Company

The history of the British East India Company is a cautionary tale of globalised corporate power that lasted from the mid-seventeenth century to the mid-nineteenth century.[12] Such chartered companies were created out of necessity as being essential for trading nations to expand markets and exploit resources. In the seventeenth century European states, such as the UK and the Netherlands, did not have the military and related resources to occupy and colonise newly discovered territories, but they had the necessary authority and power to charter private ventures and support claims to territory made by the chartered companies.[13]

The East India Company received a Charter from the Crown enabling it to exercise sovereign powers such as enter into treaties with other companies and even foreign governments,[14] to coin its own money, and to raise armies – for instance, by 1857, the British East India Company had a 250,000 strong 'sepoy' army in India led by British officers, while its main rival, the Dutch East India Company had, even as early as 1669, 150 merchant ships, forty warships, and 10,000 soldiers.[15] It was clear that the British East India Company and other similar European-based chartered companies exercised powers of government over indigenous peoples and others within their jurisdiction.[16] This is illustrated by the 1858 Government of India Act which, following the sepoy mutiny, ended British East India Company rule in India. The Act declared: 'territories under the government of the East India Company and all its property . . . were vested in the Crown, together with all the governmental powers that have previously been exercised by it'.

---

12 N. Tsagourias and N.D. White, *Collective Security: Theory, Law and Practice* (Cambridge University Press, 2013) chapter 7.

13 C. Ortiz, 'Overseas Trade in Early Modernity and the Emergence of Embryonic Private Military Companies' in Jager and Kummel (eds), *Private Military and Security Companies*, 11 at 15–16.

14 D. Kramer, 'Does History Repeat Itself? A Comparative Analysis of Private Military Entities' in Jager and Kummel, *supra* note 1, 23 at 25.

15 *Ibid.*, 27.

16 A. Anghie, *Imperialism, Sovereignty and the Making of International Law* (Oxford University Press, 2004) 68.

Such companies offered expansionist states the perfect cover of plausible deniability when ventures went wrong, and new territories, markets and revenues when things went well. Seeking out new markets, establishing trading bases, quelling local opposition by asserting authority over territories, all carried a high degree of risk, and so suited the corporate model but it had to be a violent model in order to keep indigenous populations under control and to keep rival companies at bay.[17]

Gradually the gains that colonial states made from the activities of chartered companies and other forms of private violence were outweighed by the problems they created for their national states. Privateers were essentially private ships and crews recruited during wartime and given free rein to attack and capture enemy ships as prize. But once the war was over their services were no longer needed, leading to a huge increase in piracy as they continued their activities in peacetime. Often pirates were pardoned at the outset of the next war and so become privateers again; but their activities increasingly destabilised trade, leading to the international criminalisation of pirates as *hostes humanis generis* (enemies of all humankind). By 1856, states were able to agree, in the Declaration of Paris, that 'privateering is, and remains, abolished'.

Mercenaries were gradually subsumed into the armed forces of states and then reduced as their presence in large numbers could be seen as an act of war by their state of nationality, thereby escalating conflicts often unnecessarily. By the time mercenaries were outlawed in the twentieth century,[18] their influence had been much reduced, though they enjoyed a brief renaissance during the decolonisation period in Africa.

Chartered companies were overstretched as their empires expanded, exemplified by the sepoy mutiny in India in 1857, when indigenous soldiers employed by the company rebelled against their British officers; leading to the Crown reverting to direct rule. As Thomson relates – 'mercantile companies turned their guns on each other and even on their home states'.[19] By the mid-nineteenth century the state

---

17 Ortiz, *supra* note 13, 11.
18 Art 47(2) of Additional Protocol I 1977; see slight various in definition in Art 4 OAU Convention for the Elimination of Mercenarism in Africa 1977; and Art 1 International Convention against the Recruitment, Use, Financing and Training of Mercenaries 1989.
19 Thomson, *supra* note 10, 43.

was powerful enough to assert control over the external use of force, thereby eliminating the military influence of companies, though, of course, corporate expansion in its peaceful form was encouraged, protected by the Crown and its forces.

4.5   State responsibility for private violence

In developments reminiscent of the seventeenth and eighteenth centuries, employees of corporations are once again carrying weapons in foreign conflict and post-conflict zones, as well as operating weapons systems, delivering supplies and guarding facilities. Off the coast of Somalia PMSCs provide protection to merchant ships under threat from pirates. Such armed contractors have undoubtedly used lethal force in violation of the right to life. Most infamously, Blackwater employees, engaged to protect US diplomats, shot dead seventeen Iraqi civilians in Nisour Square in Baghdad in 2007. Accountability for this violence has again been difficult to achieve. Criminal cases against Blackwater employees for manslaughter in US criminal courts are ongoing but problems of evidence and testimony will probably mean they will not result in convictions. However, a rare success was achieved in 2010 when Blackwater settled a civil case brought on behalf of victims under the US Alien Tort Statute.[20]

Contractors working for PMSCs can be engaged by other companies, non-state actors (such as the UN and non-governmental organisations (NGOs)) but some of the biggest contracts come from governments. Modern international law, with its focus on state responsibility (and increasingly on institutional responsibility) might be expected to regulate the issue of outsourcing by states and the UN so as to avoid the sort of problems private violence presented for states in the eighteenth and nineteenth centuries.

Surprisingly, international laws on state responsibility are not well-suited for this late-twentieth century phenomenon. Although the International Law Commission's (ILC's) Articles on State Responsibility were not finalised until 2001, they are clearly based on a traditional view of the state as having an exclusive hold over organised violence. A state is responsible for its organs, agents, those exercising elements

---

20 *Abtan et al v Erik Prince* available at http://www.asser.nl/upload/documents/DomCLIC/Docs/ NLP/US/Atban_complaint_10_07.pdf.

of governmental authority, and for the conduct of private individuals if 'acting on the instructions of, or under the direction or control of' the state in carrying out that conduct.[21]

Under these rules it is very difficult to directly engage the responsibility of states for wrongful acts of contractors operating under a government contract. Firstly, because contractors are not normally incorporated into the armed forces and are, therefore, not state organs. Secondly, there is an ideological disagreement about what is inherently governmental, although most states would currently see as a minimum the combat function as inherently belonging to the state. Finally, contractors do not fit the effective control test, whereby a state is responsible for the acts of private individuals, at least as the test has been developed by the ICJ in the *Nicaragua* case (1986) and the *Bosnia Genocide* case (2007).[22] This jurisprudence, read alongside Article 8 of the Articles on State Responsibility, requires the contracting state to be in effective control of the conduct of contractors, which would not normally be the case. The contract would specify the terms and conditions under which the PMSC would deliver security (for example guarding diplomats) but there would not normally be on-going control of the contractors or their conduct beyond that.

In the absence of direct state responsibility for the wrongful acts or omissions of contractors, there remains the possibility of identifying due diligence obligations on states, though it is an underdeveloped area. The idea is that contracting states (and host states and, arguably, the home state of PMSCs) should make their best efforts (by licensing, monitoring and, where necessary, punishing) to reduce the number of human rights or humanitarian law violations by PMSCs they contract with, or who are based, or operate, within their jurisdictions.[23]

The Inter-American Court of Human Rights in the *Velasquez-Rodriguez* case (1988) established the idea that states were not only directly responsible for the acts of their agents (police, army, and so on) when they violated human rights, but also for not doing enough to

---

21 Arts 4, 5 and 8, Articles on Responsibility of States for Internationally Wrongful Acts 2001.

22 *Military and Paramilitary Activities in and Against Nicaragua (Nicaragua v United States of America)* (1986) ICJ Rep, 62–4; *Application of the Convention on the Prevention and Punishment of the Crime of Genocide (Bosnia and Herzegovina v Serbia and Montenegro)* (2007) ICJ Rep, 43 at para 406.

23 N.D. White, 'Due Diligence Obligations of Conduct: Developing a Responsibility Regime for PMSCs' (2012) 31 *Criminal Justice Ethics* 233.

prevent the violation of rights by private actors.[24] That case involved the actions of shadowy death squads in 'disappearing' political activists in one of the many dirty wars in Latin America in the 1980s, but the same principle should be applicable to private armed contractors acting in violation of human rights within the jurisdiction of a state.[25]

In fulfilling these obligations under international law, states should ensure that both corporations and individuals are held responsible under national law for their violations of human rights. There are two initiatives currently being taken by different groupings of states to try and ensure that states have clear obligations as regards PMSCs, especially those they contract with, and that they accept responsibility for their wrongful acts.

The first initiative, which comes from a consortium of home states where the PMSC industry is strong and the PMSC industry itself, is known as the Montreux process. The process is based on non-binding soft law – both for states in identifying their obligations and best practice, and for corporations by developing a specific form of corporate social responsibility at the international level. The second initiative has been undertaken by the UN's Working Group on Mercenaries (which, for obvious reasons, is opposed to the privatisation of force). This seeks to regulate PMSC activities by imposing clear, binding (in other words, hard) treaty commitments on contracting host and home states, and by proposing a treaty mechanism for supervising such obligations.

4.6   Montreux process and soft law

Corporate and individual responsibility for PMSCs is to a large degree dependent on states taking their responsibilities seriously and controlling PMSCs in ways they failed to do for their predecessors in the seventeenth and eighteenth centuries. The Montreux Document of 2008 was sponsored by the Swiss government and the International Committee of the Red Cross (ICRC) and supported by the major home states of PMSCs as well as the host states.[26] It takes the form of a non-binding instrument (enabling its rapid adoption), which was

---

24 *Velasquez Rodriguez*, Ser, C No. 4 (1988), para 172.
25 See general statement of international law in *Corfu Channel Case (Merits)* (1949) ICJ Rep, 4 at 22.
26 Montreux Document on Pertinent International Legal Obligations and Good Practices for States related to Operations of Private Military and Security Companies during Armed Conflict 2008.

originally subscribed to by seventeen states. By April 2013 the number of participating states had increased to forty-four.

The Montreux Document itself points to principles of international law (mainly international humanitarian law) applicable to home, host and contracting states of PMSCs. It does little to deal with the problem of imputability to states of wrongful PMSC conduct as it adopts the orthodox narrow vision of state responsibility identified above, but its good practices (including supporting the idea of national licensing schemes for PMSCs) could be seen through a due diligence lens, although they are not crafted as clear obligations upon states. In addition to its narrow focus on armed conflict and its non-binding nature, the Montreux Document contains no mechanisms for supervision or enforcement.

The Montreux Document created a framework for states but did not apply to PMSCs, when ideally a combination of state and corporate responsibility is needed, so an outgrowth from it was the adoption of the International Code of Conduct for Security Providers of 2010. The Code of Conduct is built on the concept of corporate social responsibility developed most fully, at least for multinational corporations, by John Ruggie, the UN Secretary General's Special Rapporteur for Business and Human Rights. Ruggie's 'protect, respect, remedy' framework places clear international legal obligations on states, which must act to ensure that human rights abuses are not committed by private parties (the protect element); while corporations should avoid infringing the human rights of others (the respect element); and, finally, there should be access to justice for victims of abuse (the remedy element).[27]

While states bear international legal obligations to ensure that companies act in accordance with international law, companies are expected to reduce the prospect of state intervention by developing corporate social responsibility regimes. If corporations are diligent in respecting human rights, then the due diligence obligations of states become less onerous.

The International Code of Conduct is one of the most advanced of its type and specifically applies to private security providers. By April

---

27 J. Ruggie, 'Guiding Principles on Businesses and Human Rights: Implementing the United Nations "Protect, Respect and Remedy" Framework', UN Doc A/HRC/17/31, 21 March 2011; endorsed by the UN's Human Rights Council in UN Doc A/HRC/RES/17/4 (2011).

2013, 602 companies had signed up to the Code. Although it is not binding on PMSCs the Code does detail the human rights that PMSCs are expected to respect (including restrictions on the use of force and torture). Further, it requires PMSCs to exercise due diligence in vetting and training of employees as well as having grievance procedures and effective remedies to victims of abuse.

An oversight mechanism for the Code was agreed in February 2013 by a small consortium of states, industry and civil society organisations, under which representatives of each constituency will form an association and be responsible for 'certifying that a company's systems and policies meet the Code's principles and the standards derived from the Code and that a company is undergoing monitoring, auditing, and verification, including in the field'; and for 'exercising external independent oversight of member companies' performance under the Code, including through monitoring, reporting and a process to address alleged violations of the code'. The association is empowered to request a member company take corrective action to remedy non-compliance with the Code within a specified time period. A non-compliant company may suffer suspension or termination of membership.[28]

The strengths and weaknesses of the association are readily apparent, especially the danger of the Board being dominated by a small section of states and industry representatives, and that the sanctions at its disposal have not been proven to be effective in other codes of conduct. Nevertheless, the operation of the association will determine whether it is a robust mechanism of oversight and accountability, or more of a symbolic form of corporate social responsibility.

4.7   Draft convention for the regulation of PMSCs

The alternative initiative to address the accountability gaps that arise with the increase in contracting out of security services is the attempt to produce a binding treaty, to which states (and, innovatively, organisations such as the UN) could become parties. The Draft Convention put forward to the Human Rights Council by the UN Working Group on Mercenaries in 2010 incorporates a strong approach to inherent state functions, not only by having a long list of such functions as

---

28 Arts 10–12, Articles of Association, International Code of Conduct for Private Security Providers' Association 2013.

performed by PMSCs, but also by prohibiting the outsourcing of such functions by governments.[29] This position contrasts with the premises underlying the ILC Articles on State Responsibility of 2011, where the position seems to be that, although governmental functions can be outsourced, responsibility for those functions cannot.[30]

Nonetheless, the discussion of what can be outsourced and what cannot is not simply about law but about the very essence of statehood. This can be illustrated by pointing out one of the differences between the International Code of Conduct of 2010 and the Draft Convention of the same year. The International Code of Conduct assumes that PMSC personnel have the right to carry weapons as well as to use them in different forms of self-defence, although the Code does require PMSCs to have authorisations for the possession and use of any weapons as required by applicable law.[31] In this way the Codes' provisions on the use of force seem compatible with the state's monopoly on violence since the possession of weapons and the use of force by PMSCs have to be in accordance with national law.

Although the Draft Convention's provisions on the use of force overlap with the Code of Conduct, especially on defining the right of self-defence,[32] there are two fundamental differences. The Draft Convention prohibits the outsourcing of law enforcement functions,[33] thereby prohibiting the use of force by PMSCs in pursuit of law enforcement; and, secondly, it strongly emphasises the application of non-violent means before resort to firearms.[34] The differences between the Draft Convention and the International Code of Conduct reflect different philosophies on the limitations upon outsourcing and the monopoly on the use of force.

If adopted, the Draft Convention, would have a number of advantages over the Montreux Document in that it would contain clear binding obligations on home, host and contracting states and contracting organisations by, inter alia, requiring each to adopt legislative and

29 In Report of the Working Group on the Use of Mercenaries as a Means of Violating Human Rights and Impeding the Exercise of the Right to Self-Determination, UN Doc A/HRC/15/25, 2 July 2010.

30 Art 5, Articles on the Responsibility of States for Internationally Wrongful Acts of State 2001.

31 International Code of Conduct for Private Security Providers 2010, para 56.

32 Draft Convention on the Regulation of PMSCs 2010, Art 18(4).

33 Ibid., Art 9.

34 Ibid., Art 18(2).

administrative measures to regulate and, if necessary, punish PMSCs and individual contractors when violations occur, and to have licensing systems. The inclusion in the Draft Convention of a strong oversight mechanism based on a Committee of independent experts review-ing and critiquing state reports and allowing for state and individual complaints would give the Convention real teeth and help ensure that states and organisations actually fulfil their due diligence obligations. The Oversight Committee would, over time, develop clear standards that would fill in the general due diligence obligations that, arguably, give too much discretion to states.

At the time of writing the Draft Convention was undergoing re-negoti-ation and change in an Open Ended Working Group of states set up by the Human Rights Council. It remains doubtful whether it will see the light of day, but without such a treaty, containing strong supervisory mechanisms, states will not see the need to properly control PMSCs until, as with their predecessors the chartered companies, the disad-vantages of uncontrolled private violence outweigh the benefits.

4.8   Lessons of history

History shows us that state sovereignty is rarely absolute. Arguably only the nineteenth and early twentieth centuries saw the absolute state in which (at least powerful) states controlled violence externally as well as internally. Problems of unconstrained private violence wit-nessed in the seventeenth and eighteenth centuries have arisen again, where private contractors have violated international law, for example the right to life in Nisour Square and the right to freedom from tor-ture in Abu Ghraib. However, international legal mechanisms are not robust enough to hold either the companies, contractors or the states contracting for their services to account.

The key, certainly for international law, is for states to exercise greater control over PMSCs in fulfilment of their due diligence obligations under international human rights law (and in other applicable areas of international law such as international humanitarian law). This neces-sitates the development of mechanisms of state (and institutional) responsibility by means of supervised treaty obligations requiring states to have proper national licensing systems. Furthermore, states should accept responsibility for acts done in performance of inherent state functions, so agreement on a core of inherently governmental functions (combat, arrest and detention, interrogation) should be achievable. For PMSCs, corporate social responsibility is essential since it will only be by means of a combination of state, corporate and individual responsibility that proper accountability and access to justice for corporate human rights abuses will be possible.

5 Collective security law

5.1 Introduction

Collective security is simply the idea, arguably the ideal, whereby all states will contribute, normally through an international organisation, collectively to combat aggression and threats to peace and security.[1] This might be done by diplomacy, non-forcible or forcible means. Of course, in the case of aggression, the ideal breaks down, partially since at least one state will be acting in violation of international norms, which may result in a collective security response where all, or some, remaining states confront the aggression and deal with the threat, or it may lead to a response from the attacked state in self-defence, possibly joined by its allies to help it in collective self-defence.

While the formal rules of the UN Charter restrict actions in individual or collective self-defence to responses to 'armed attacks',[2] realists and other pragmatists would argue that self-defence should not be so formally defined but should be seen in the context of protecting national interests and achieving a balance of power between states. Thus, while a formalist interpretation of the UN Charter would see the US imposition of a quarantine around Cuba in 1962, in response to the positioning of Soviet nuclear missiles, as an unjustified threat and use of force since there was no (imminent) armed attack against the US from Cuba; a more pragmatic response would view it as a proportionate response to a threat to US national interests in the context of a global Cold War between the US and the USSR.

---

1 See generally G.W. Downs, *Collective Security beyond the Cold War* (University of Michigan Press, 1994) 1–16.
2 Art 51 UN Charter.

In 1996 Martti Koskenniemi published an influential article on 'The Place of Law in Collective Security',[3] in which he effectively debunked the realist claim to accurately describe (and, moreover, predict) social practices. Despite the indeterminacy of international law, which is at its most extreme in the area of high politics in which collective security is located, Koskenniemi argued powerfully that norms, more specifically laws, have a significant role in collective security: firstly because Realism itself contains within it normative understandings of key concepts such as 'interest' (as in the national interest), 'security' (as in national security) and 'power' (as in balance of power); and, secondly, because the legal justifications put forward by states for their actions were not simply excuses but meaningful justifications and explanations for action.[4]

According to Koskenniemi, when the political framework is stable law plays a pragmatic role, for example, in shaping the text of Security Council resolutions; but when the framework is unstable the Charter (and international security law) becomes central in shaping the boundary between law and politics. Law is a constraint on discretion, not in a fully 'constitutional' sense, but in a 'political' sense.[5]

In the first half of this chapter this argument will be used to confront resurgent pragmatism (as practised for instance by the US and expertly articulated by Michael Glennon), but also as a route into collective (and changing) legal and political understandings of both 'collective' and 'security'. This will lead to an assessment of the normative function of collective security law and its relationship to the efficacy of collective security.

In the second half of this chapter the legal highpoint of discussions in and around the UN Security Council in Iraq in 1990, following the breakdown of the stable political framework of the Cold War, will be used as a starting point to map the relationship between law and politics in the Security Council in the post-Cold War era. Did the new political framework (the 'war on terror') after 9/11 in 2001 represent another highpoint (or otherwise) for collective security law? More

---

3   M. Koskenniemi, 'The Place of Law in Collective Security' (1996) 17 *Michigan Journal of International Law* 455.

4   *Ibid.*, 465, 469, 472, 476. For a realist account see A.V. Levotin, *The Myth of International Security: A Juridical and Critical Analysis* (Oxford University Press, 1957).

5   Koskenniemi, *supra* note 3, 473, 478, 480.

generally, has international law settled back into being a handmaiden to pragmatism in collective security or does it somehow play an external role to politics, challenging and perhaps controlling politics despite being inside social practices?

5.2   Security communities

The overall argument to be considered in this chapter is whether understanding the role of law in collective security can (or, indeed, does) empower the security community (of states and organisations) to increase law's relevance to political decision-making on security matters? Some preliminary evidence suggests a positive answer: the UN's response to 9/11 was not the same as that of the US, and the latter's insistence on its 'right' to continue to prosecute some form of 'war' against terror or terrorists has not been accepted, indeed, it has increasingly been seen as 'wrong'.

Karl Deutsch, who considered various historical arrangements of states that succeeded in removing conflict within their membership, defined a 'security community' in 1957 as 'one in which there is a real assurance that the members of that community will not fight each other physically, but will settle their disputes in some other way'. He went on to say that 'if the entire world were integrated as a security-community, wars would be automatically eliminated'. By integration, he did not necessarily mean amalgamation into one state, rather the attainment of a 'sense of community and of institutions and practices strong enough and widespread enough to assure for a long time, dependable expectations of peaceful change'.[6] It is 'whenever states become integrated to the point that they have a sense of community', that the 'assurance that they will settle their differences short of war' is created.[7] Community building is a product of 'shared understandings, transnational values and transaction flows'. Once established, a security community generates stable expectations of peaceful change.[8]

---

6 K. Deutsch, *Political Community and the North Atlantic Area: International Organization in the Light of Historical Experience* (New York: Greenwood, 1957) 5–6.

7 E. Adler and M. Barnett, 'Security Communities in Theoretical Perspective' in E. Adler and M. Barnett, (eds), *Security Communities* (Cambridge University Press, 1998) 4.

8 *Ibid.*, 4–6.

Although the UN collective security organisation has not completely matched Karl Deutsch's concept of a security community, as evidenced by the continuation of regular and frequent conflicts in the post-1945 world order, it has helped humankind to achieve the basic condition of any security community – survival.[9] There is evidence that the UN emerged from the Second World War as a form of 'security community'.

Ian Brownlie considers that the prosecution of the Second World War by the Allies against the Axis powers went beyond collective defence and became a war of sanction, the purpose of which was to remove a danger to world peace by extirpating the source of aggression. He states that such a war of sanction in the UN period, if not 'an organized community action', no longer has any place. Indeed, he links the prosecution of the Second World War to the UN, even though the organisation was not formally created until the war's end, by considering that the 'majority of states entered the war against the Axis powers on the basis of the United Nations Declaration of 1942 and the Moscow Declaration of 1943'. While 'collective defence by a large number of states may have the appearance of a war of sanction . . . the legal powers of states exercising the right of collective defence are restricted' by the requirements of self-defence, particularly proportionality.[10] Following this line of argument, a security community was created in 1945 when the UN was established, but its origins can be traced back to 1942, when the Allied powers proclaimed themselves the 'United Nations' in order to defend themselves from Axis aggressors, then to defeat them completely and shape a global peace.[11]

The UN certainly was a much improved collective security organisation when compared to the League of Nations, with the founding states of the UN collectively giving the smaller 'executive' or 'governing body', the Security Council of fifteen states (increased from eleven in 1965), significant powers in the realm of restoring or maintaining international peace and security. The Security Council's powers are specified under Chapters VI and VII of the UN Charter, with the former containing a range of recommendatory powers in relation to the peaceful settlement of disputes or situations that might endanger the peace,

---

9 Deutsch, *supra* note 6, 3.

10 I. Brownlie, *Principles of Public International Law* (7th edn, Oxford University Press, 2008) 332–3.

11 But see J.W. Wheeler-Bennett and A. Nicholls, *The Semblance of Peace: The Political Settlement After the Second World War* (London: Macmillan, 1972) 528–53.

including fact-finding and recommending methods of adjustment or terms of settlement.[12] The powers contained in Chapter VII, to demand provisional measures such as cease-fires, to take a range of non-forcible measures including economic sanctions, and to take military action,[13] are contingent upon the Council making a determination of a 'threat to the peace', 'breach of the peace' or 'act of aggression'.[14] The Security Council has certainly adopted an expansive interpretation of 'threat to the peace' to include not only threats of force and threats to inter-state security but also to cover internal violence and conflicts which have the potential to spill over into neighbouring states, as well as threats from terrorists and pirates.[15]

The concentration of power in the hands of the Security Council has led to a continuing debate as to where competence lies, if at all, if the Council is unable to act due to collective inaction or, as was the case during the Cold War, due to the pernicious use of the veto. While the voting rules of the Security Council were an improvement on the requirements of unanimity in the League of Nations' Covenant,[16] they still require consensus within the P5.[17]

The veto was so prevalent during the Cold War, initially primarily by the Soviet Union (who cast its veto seventy-seven times in the first ten years of the UN) and later by the US, that the UN was often reduced to a bystander (as during the war in Vietnam 1959–1975) or, at best, a forum for diplomacy between the superpowers (for example during the Cuban Missile Crisis of 1962). The presence of the veto signifies that the Security Council should not be viewed simply as an 'instrument of action' rather, as Inis Claude pointed out, its basic function is as a forum for negotiation and diplomacy.[18] Thus, it is fallacious to argue that the UN has failed simply because it was unable to take action against the US and Soviet Union during the Cuban Missile

---

12 Arts 34, 36, 37, 38 UN Charter.

13 Arts 40, 41, 42 UN Charter.

14 Art 39 UN Charter.

15 For example UNSC Res 1373 (2001) re terrorism, and UNSC Res 1846 (2008) re piracy. See generally C. Henderson, 'The Centrality of the United Nations Security Council in the Legal Regime Governing the Use of Force' in N.D. White and C. Henderson (eds), *Research Handbook on International Conflict and Security Law* (Cheltenham: Edward Elgar Publishing, 2013) 120.

16 Art 5 Covenant of the League of Nations 1919.

17 Art 27(3) of the UN Charter requires decisions to be 'made by an affirmative vote of nine [originally seven] members including the concurring votes of the permanent members'.

18 I. Claude, 'The Security Council' in E. Luard (ed.), *The Evolution of International Organization* (London: Thames and Hudson, 1966) 68 at 83–8.

Crisis. The UN still served as a forum for negotiation between the two superpowers, enabling both to climb down from their position of near nuclear confrontation. If the Council fails to fulfil even its basic function as a forum for diplomacy then it can be argued that it has not carried out its primary role for the maintenance of international peace and security as placed upon it by the UN Charter,[19] and authority must therefore pass to another security community, either to the UN General Assembly or, arguably, to established and competent regional security organisations.

5.3   Collective security in the Cold War

Even when the Security Council managed to agree on a resolution during the Cold War, law played a secondary role to politics. A good example is Resolution 242, adopted following the Six Day War of 1967, when Israel captured large tracts of territory in pre-emptive military operations against its Arab neighbours. In part the Resolution read that the Security Council:

> Affirms that the fulfilment of Charter principles requires the establishment of a just and lasting peace in the Middle East which should include the application of both the following principles:
>
> (i)   Withdrawal of Israeli armed forces from territories occupied in the recent conflict;
>
> (ii)   Termination of all claims or states of belligerency and respect for and acknowledgement of the sovereignty, territorial integrity and political independence of every State in the area and their right to live in peace within secure and recognised boundaries free from threats or acts of force.

Although Resolution 242 appeared to be built upon respect for fundamental principles of international law – the non-use of force, territorial integrity and sovereignty – the desire to keep Israel engaged with the peace process meant law played a secondary role to the politics of peace, since the Resolution did not make it clear that Israel should withdraw from 'all' the occupied territories, an interpretation Israel has followed to this day. Moreover, the Resolution contains no reference

---

19 Art 24(1) UN Charter.

of the Palestinian right to self-determination, although this right has clearly been recognised by other organs in the UN system.[20]

Early debates in the Security Council revolved around formal inter-pretations of the Charter's provisions. For instance, in 1946 the Security Council established a sub-committee of five members to con-sider whether the survival of a fascist regime in Europe (Spain under General Franco) was a danger to international peace within the sense of Chapter VI of the Charter, or a threat to the peace within the mean-ing of Chapter VII,[21] as if the two could be distinguished normatively and not just politically.[22]

However, concern with identifying with precision highly opaque terms in the UN Charter soon turned to exploring and sometimes exploit-ing those ambiguities. The veto prevented the Council from being an organ of military action during the Cold War, with one glaring exception, following the North Korean invasion of the South in 1950. Although the US was prepared to intervene in favour of the South on the basis of collective self-defence, the greater legitimacy (and freedom of action) that a Security Council mandate would give led the US to exploit the absence of the Soviet Union from the Council's chamber (in protest at the fact that the Chinese permanent seat was occupied by the Nationalist government and not the Communist one). In these unique circumstances the remaining members of the Security Council were able to adopt a resolution that recommended that states assist-ing South Korea repel the attack and 'restore international peace and security in the area'.[23]

The legal argument for being able to adopt a resolution even though one of the permanent members was not present was that this should be treated as an abstention, which in Security Council practice had not been treated as a veto.[24] Clearly this was a justificatory argument that is difficult to reconcile with the text of Article 27, which required concur-ring votes from all the permanent members. Furthermore, the formal

---

20 For example UNGA Res 3414 (1975).

21 UNSC Res 4 (1946); Report of the Sub-Committee on the Spanish Question (1946), 4–5.

22 N.D. White, *Keeping the Peace: The United Nations and the Maintenance of International Peace and Security* (2nd edn, Manchester University Press, 1997) 36–42.

23 UNSC Res 83 (1950).

24 This was finally recognised by the ICJ in *Legal Consequences for States of the Continued Presence of South Africa in Namibia (South West Africa) Notwithstanding Security Council 276 (1970)*, (1971) ICJ Rep 16.

provisions of Chapter VII, which require UN forces to be deployed on the basis of pre-existing agreements between states and the UN, combined with a form of UN command and control centred in the Military Staff Committee,[25] were brushed to one side in favour of a very loose mandate given to a US-led coalition when command and control was delegated to the US and so was the competence to restore international peace.

Finally, when the Soviet Union returned and no further resolutions were possible in the Council, the UK insisted that the US-led operation gain authority from the UN General Assembly to cross over the thirty-eighth parallel which had divided the two Koreas since Japanese withdrawal at the end of the Second World War.[26] This marked one of the highpoints of the General Assembly's still controversial claim to be a security community.

The political constraints on the Council that had solidified even by 1950 led to legal interpretations of the Charter that would have made most domestic lawyers blush: ignoring the voting roles, brushing aside the carefully crafted provisions on the most sensitive aspect of the Security Council's tools of action – military forces – and, finally, transferring competence in what appeared to be almost a cavalier fashion to the General Assembly when the Soviet veto returned to the Council. However, by 1953 when the war ended, it seemed to be the accepted orthodoxy in the UN that the Korean War had been prosecuted by the US-led coalition on behalf of the UN.[27] Law followed politics in 1950, but in 1990, when the end of the Cold War made confronting aggression possible again, law came to shape politics (reviewed in the next section).

As with forcible measures, those rare non-forcible measures that were possible during the Cold War were shaped by political considerations not by law: law was relevant in terms of the binding and overriding nature of sanctions regimes,[28] but also in justifying the choice of constitutional path in a shared understanding within the UN Security Council that such measures could be taken under Chapter VII to

---

25 Arts 43 and 47 UN Charter.

26 UNGA Res 376 (1950).

27 See UNSG Trygve Lie in UN Doc A/1287 (1950).

28 Arts 25 and 103 of the UN Charter.

address essentially internal situations where there was a denial of self-determination and human rights by racists regimes.[29]

The system of apartheid in South Africa and other repressive policies of the white racist regime led to the imposition of an arms embargo against South Africa in 1977,[30] but only after the regime had become self-sufficient in arms. The Unilateral Declaration of Independence from the UK by the white minority regime in Southern Rhodesia in 1965 led to more comprehensive and hurtful sanctions, although these were breached with impunity by, amongst others, the US.[31] The comprehensive sanctions model was again used as a precedent in the Council, once the shackles of the Cold War were thrown off, when it was faced with Iraq's invasion and occupation of Kuwait in 1990.

5.4 Law as central to collective security?

According to Koskenniemi law took on a shaping role in the 1990 crisis that followed the Iraqi invasion of Kuwait. The end of the Cold War meant that:

> The traditional patterns of Council decision-making had become irrelevant and inapplicable. There was no anterior political agreement, no longstanding negotiation with fixed positions, and no routine language to cover events. The situation was canvassed nowhere but in the Charter itself. As the debate took on a legal style and an engaged aspect, the rest of formalism followed suit.[32]

This took place, for example, in the search for legal precedent in the management of sanctions where Rhodesia was clearly the template, while the mandating resolution for force in 1950 against North Korea was used as the template for Resolution 678 (1990), which authorised member states to enforce the Security Council's demand for Iraqi withdrawal and 'to restore international peace and security to the area'.

---

29 Art 2(7) of the UN Charter. See generally M.E. O'Connell, 'Debating the Law of Sanctions', (2002) 13 *EJIL* 63.

30 UNSC Res 418 (1977).

31 UNSC Res 232 (1966); UNSC Res 253 (1968). There was a limited enforcement of these sanctions by the UK in the Beira patrol authorised in UNSC Res 221 (1966).

32 Koskenniemi, *supra* note 3, 476–7.

However, the move to law was evidenced in the way these precedents were put together with other legally-based responses in a suite of resolutions whereby the Council used the full range of its Chapter VII powers in an incremental way in 1990. It started with a determination of a breach of the peace under Article 39 and a demand for Iraqi withdrawal under Article 40 (in Resolution 660), imposed sanctions under Article 41 (Resolution 661), determined that Iraq's annexation of Kuwait was null and void (Resolution 662), authorised naval force to enforce sanctions in a limited application of Article 42 (Resolution 665), then an authorisation to use full-scale force to remove Iraq (Resolution 678), and many resolutions in between.

There was even discussion, for the first time in the UN's history, of the relationship between the Security Council's response and Kuwait's right to individual and collective self-defence.[33] This arose because US and UK forces started to gather in the Gulf at the request of the deposed government of Kuwait on the basis of Article 51 of the Charter, prior to the adoption of Resolution 678 (which was implicitly based on Article 42). The debate was heightened by the fact that Article 51 formally seems to end the right of self-defence once the Security Council has taken measures necessary to restore peace and security, leading to debate as to whether sanctions could be deemed to be such measures,[34] although the point became moot once the Council adopted Resolution 678, which participating states then used as the legal basis for prosecuting the war against Iraq that led to its defeat in 1991.[35] The conflict was ended by the Security Council in 1991: first with a temporary cease-fire (Resolution 686) and then a resolution which imposed draconian conditions upon Iraq: disarmament, boundary settlement, and compensation – all to be enforced by the continuation of economic sanctions against Iraq and an elaborate inspection regime (Resolution 687).

The consensus within the P5 enabled the Council to develop a legal framework for its post-war actions (implicitly under Article 41's open-ended list of non-forcible measures) that would have been unimaginable during the Cold War. However, that consensus had dissipated by

---

33 N.D. White, 'From Korea to Kuwait: The Legal Basis of United Nations Military Action' (1998) 20 *The International History Review* 597 at 610–12. But see O. Schachter, 'United Nations Law in the Gulf' (1991) *AJIL* 459–60.

34 UNSC 2937 meeting (1990).

35 White, *supra* note 33, 615–17.

2003, with the US, the UK and, at least to start with, France, bridling against Iraq's perceived lack of compliance, especially with the disarmament provisions, leading to increasing unilateral enforcement by military means culminating in the full-scale invasion of Iraq by the US and the UK in 2003.

By 2003 law once again took a back seat to politics, evidenced by the unconvincing attempts by the UK in particular to justify the use of force against Iraq in 2003 on the basis that Resolution 678 of 1990 was still a valid authorisation to use force. The 'revival' argument, as it came to be known, only came to the fore once it became clear that a follow-up resolution that would enforce the inspection regime re-established by Resolution 1441 (2002) was not going to be achieved due to French and Russian reticence – at least to agree to the timetable set by the US and the UK to coincide with the build-up of their military forces.

Military and political conditions dictated that the invasion of Iraq would take place in March 2003 but without a valid authorising resolution from the Security Council. In these circumstances the UK argued that a material breach of Resolution 1441's obligations by Iraq for full disclosure and cooperation was traceable back to the disarmament obligations found in Resolution 687 that ended the war in 1991. The UK contended Resolution 687 only suspended and did not terminate the authority to use force in Resolution 678.[36] The US supported this argument without any real enthusiasm,[37] preferring instead to see this as an issue of its security. When debates in the Security Council were going against a second resolution in early March 2003 – a resolution that would have authorised force – President Bush declared that 'we don't really need the United Nations' approval to act . . . when it comes to our security, we do not need anyone's permission'.[38] Iraq in 2003, unlike Iraq in 1990, appeared to mark a return to pragmatism but was it really a return to pragmatism?

---

36 See Parliamentary Written Answer to House of Lords given by the Attorney General Lord Goldsmith, *Hansard* HL, Vol 646, WA2-3, 17 March 2003.

37 In a document submitted to the Security Council – UN Doc S/2003/215 (2003).

38 In R. Cornwell, 'The Quiet Man' *Independent*, 8 March 2003, 3.

5.5   Return to pragmatism?

Michael Glennon argues that pragmatism is, and has been, the better explanation and approach to international law. Pragmatists, he argues are 'legal realists who believe that what ostensibly are background considerations inevitably affect legalist decision-making; that reliance upon formal legal categories masks the decision-making process that actually occurs, which is situationally contingent'.[39]

As a method it certainly seems to describe the failures of attempts at collective security, at least as occurred over Iraq in 2003, better than any theoretical or doctrinal depiction of collective security as a set of authoritative institutions and controlling rules. Glennon points out that not only are the formal rules largely irrelevant to state behaviour, especially in the areas of high politics purportedly regulated by collective security law and institutions, but further, that there are no foundational principles upon which a legal order can be constructed.[40] He uses this to reject any notion of a moral basis for action, any concept of hierarchy in international law embodied in notions of *jus cogens*, as well as any purportedly abstract concepts such as 'community' or 'justice'.[41]

Realists thus reject the 'paper rules' found in the Charter and in other treaties (both those rules governing the use of force and those purportedly regulating collective security organs) and in the distillation of custom by positivist international lawyers or judges, in favour of the working rules that are observable empirically and do actually work in terms of inducing compliance.[42]

While superficially attractive the pragmatist has effectively collapsed any distinction between law and politics, between breach and compliance. The UN did fail to agree on action in 2003, but the pragmatist's analysis only describes the policies and actions of those that wanted to use force. A pragmatic analysis will usually shed light on the complexities of politics and power that go into decision-making processes, but this does not reveal the law, at least if we ascribe any autonomous

---

39 M.J. Glennon, *The Fog of Law: Pragmatism, Security, and International Law* (Stanford University Press, 2010) 3.

40 *Ibid.*, 5.

41 *Ibid.*

42 *Ibid.*, 27.

function to the 'law'. The real 'rules' of the pragmatist are not rules at all but wholly contingent explanations of behaviour.

The fact that the US used force in Iraq in 2003 out of self-interest and perceptions of threats to its security (and out of a sense of a job unfinished in 1991, and a vague idea that 9/11 and Iraq were related), and not out of a belief in the revival argument as a valid exception to the ban on the use of force, is not a 'rule' in any sense other than that any act of unpunished violence creates an argument that can be wielded against those that insist on a formal application of the law.

The only rules in a realist analysis that emerge are those as defined by the realist – that power and self-interest explain action. In effect the pragmatist replaces one set of foundations (based on *jus cogens* and other basic principles and purposes of international law) with normative foundations of another kind based on power and self-interest. Real rules are so contingent as to be impossible to formulate in any meaningful sense, resulting in a case-by-case analysis where any lessons learned cannot be put forward as universal rules.[43] Legal principles may be weak in comparison to these real 'rules' but given that the latter is just a short-hand term for power and self-interest, the formal laws remain as constraints, no matter how weak, on power. To conflate power and law is to remove law from having any independent function from power, including arguably its key function – as a restraint on power. Thus, the realist analysis of law is in itself a self-serving argument that attempts to replace law in any normative sense with power and self-interest.

It may well be very difficult to prove that most states do not use force because of a formal legal principle prohibiting force in the UN Charter,[44] but constant restatement of that principle by organs of the international community such as the General Assembly must indicate that the formal rule is and will be a factor that determines state behaviour. The alleged failure of the Security Council to fully adapt to the changed conditions of Iraq in 2003 does not mean that it has been irrelevant since its creation in 1945 when geopolitics were very different.[45] The Council did adapt in 1990; besides which, it is equally plausible to argue that the Security Council's inability to authorise

---

43 *Ibid.*, 122–3.
44 *Ibid.*, 89.
45 But see *ibid.*, 163: 'the world today is saddled with the outmoded institutions of a bygone era'.

force in 2003 was because the weight of world opinion was behind the threatened vetoes of France and Russia and not behind those states (the US and the UK) agitating to go to war. In other words the Council, by its inability to authorise force, reflected contemporary thinking on the rules governing when force should be used, meaning that the use of force by the US and the UK was not somehow lawful, as the pragmatists would argue, but is what most believe it to be – an illegal use of force.

The invasion of Iraq in 2003 can be convincingly analysed in terms of law's survival and continued independence from politics; but the fact remains (and this is the ultimate pragmatic argument) that the US and the UK got away with it. In response to this one can point to the problems both countries had in imposing their will on Iraq after the invasion, despite having Security Council approval for their occupation and state building (itself a legal contradiction since the law of occupation is antithetical to state-building),[46] since that initial intervention in breach of the *jus ad bellum* undermined the justice of their cause when trying to rebuild Iraq.

The response of the UN's organs to the attack on the US of 9/11 in 2001 also illustrates the continued role of law in providing a counter-point to the raw politics of power. The Security Council, while generally being behind the US, did not fully endorse its right of self-defence in response to the attack. Resolution 1368 adopted on 12 September 2001 recognised the right of individual or collective self-defence under the Charter and condemned the terrorist attacks on the US, which it regarded as a threat to international peace and security, something short of an authorisation to use force or even an endorsement of the US's right of self-defence. This may well have been because the evidence had not yet been gathered as to al-Qaeda's (and Afghanistan's) responsibility, but this in itself shows a due deference to law. Furthermore, while the UN Security Council has been willing to authorise the NATO-led International Security Assistance Force (ISAF) operation to provide security in Afghanistan,[47] this has been kept legally separate from the continuing US claim to be acting in self-defence against al-Qaeda, which has a dubious pedigree given that self-defence in any legal system is a temporary condition necessitated by the exigencies of fending off an attack. The General Assembly also on

---

46 UNSC Res 1483 (2003).
47 UNSC Res 1386 (2001).

12 September 2001 strongly condemned the heinous acts of terrorism and called for cooperation to bring the perpetrators to justice and for holding those supporting terrorism to be held accountable,[48] thereby expressing preference for a criminal justice, rather than a military, response to terrorism.

By not endorsing the legal reconstruction of the right of self-defence and law of war in the so-called 'war on terror', the UN has reinforced the role of law as a constraint on power. While the US has continued to use drones to kill suspected terrorists and has continued to detain 'unlawful combatants' in Guantanamo, the criticism of these actions as violations of human rights law and international humanitarian law has isolated it in the world community. Yes it has got away with these violations of the *jus ad bellum* and the *jus in bello* but there has been no acceptance that this makes it right.[49]

In its non-forcible measures against the Taliban and al-Qaeda, in the form of targeted sanctions aimed at cutting off funding to terrorists and terrorist organisations,[50] the Security Council has grudgingly brought its regime more into line with human rights law due to the criticism of authoritative legal organs – principally the Human Rights Committee, the European Court of Justice and the ECtHR – that targeted sanctions violated rights to privacy, freedom of movement, due process and right to a remedy.[51] Although the creation of an ombudsperson by the Security Council in 2009 falls short of providing a full judicial remedy for those wishing to claim wrongful listing, it goes a long way towards this and will provide a remedy in many cases.[52] The creation of such a body is unprecedented in the history of the Security Council and, as such, is recognition that the Security Council takes its human rights responsibilities into account when formulating and reformulating collective security measures.

---

48 UNGA 56/1 (2001).
49 For an excellent discussion of the legal issues (of the use of force, international humanitarian law and human rights law) see E.S. Bates, *Terrorism and International Law: Accountability, Remedies, and Reform (A Report of the IBA Task Force on Terrorism)* (Oxford University Press, 2011) 38–51.
50 UNSC Res 1267 (1998).
51 *Sayadi and Vinck v Belgium* (2009) 16 IHRR 16 at para 10.11 (Human Rights Committee); Joined Cases C-402/05 P and C-415/05 P *Kadi and Al Barakaat International Foundation v Council for the European Union* [2008] ECR I-6351, paras 324, 352 (European Court of Justice); *Nada v Switzerland*, Application No. 10593/08, 12 September 2012 (European Court of Human Rights).
52 UNSC Res 1904 (2009). See K. Prost, 'Fair Process and the Security Council: A Case for the Office of the Ombudsperson' in A.M. Salinas, K. Samuel, and N.D. White (eds), *Counter-Terrorism: International Law and Practice* (Oxford University Press, 2012) 409.

The General Assembly has also played a role in pointing out states' legal obligations and the Security Council's broader responsibilities in the age of terror. In formulating its Global Counter-Terrorism Strategy of 2006, the General Assembly reflects the consensus among states that collective security approaches to counter-terrorism must be human rights compliant.[53] The Strategy develops many of the measures of its earlier Declarations, but also takes account of Security Council resolutions and mechanisms, including the Counter Terrorism Committee established by Security Council Resolution 1373 to ensure that states comply with their obligations to prevent terrorist financing under that resolution (although the Assembly calls on the Committee to work with states at their request). It also recognises the role of the 1267 Committee, established by Security Council Resolution 1267, which oversees the listing and implementation of sanctions against members of al-Qaeda and the Taliban (although the Assembly calls on the Committee to ensure fair and transparent procedures). This amounts to a general recognition of the Security Council's actions in this area, but also represents an attempt to balance the Council's actions with human rights protection, and to emphasise traditional principles such as state consent.

In fact, even during the law-sparse era of the Cold War the General Assembly played an important role as the conscience of the world community as well as the Security Council, regularly condemning superpower breaches of international law – for example by the Soviet Union for its invasions of Hungary in 1956 and Afghanistan in 1979,[54] and the US for its hemispheric interventions, for example in Grenada in 1983 and Panama in 1989,[55] as well as regularly condemning its punitive and vindictive embargo of Cuba.[56] Koskenniemi describes the Assembly as the temple of justice and warns against the Security Council taking on the mantle of justice as this would let the police into the temple of justice.[57] Unfortunately, this has not prevented the Security Council from deciding on issues of justice, or at least setting up mechanisms, for example, the *ad hoc* criminal tribunals to deliver justice in Rwanda and Yugoslavia.[58] This in turn leads to a considera-

---

53 UNGA Res 60/288 (2006).

54 UNGA Res 1004 (1956); UNGA Res ES-6/2 (1980).

55 UNGA Res 38/7 (1983); UNGA Res 44/240 (1989).

56 UNGA Res 67/4 (2012).

57 M. Koskenniemi, 'The Police in the Temple Order, Justice and the UN: A Dialectical View' (1995) 6 *EJIL* 325.

58 UNSC Res 827 (1993); UNSC Res 955 (1994).

tion of whether the Assembly itself could, indeed should, take on a policing role.

5.6   Subsidiary collective security responsibility

As the ICJ stated in the *Expenses* case in 1962, when considering the constitutionality of peacekeeping forces mandated by the General Assembly, the Security Council is given primary responsibility for international peace and security (in Article 24 of the UN Charter), not exclusive responsibility, so that the Assembly was competent to recommend peacekeeping forces be deployed with the consent of the host state in Egypt in 1956 and the Congo in 1960.[59] On both occasions the Security Council was deadlocked by vetoes – British and French in the case of Suez and the Soviet Union in the instance of the Congo.

On both occasions the issue was passed from the Security Council to the General Assembly under the auspices of a procedure for invoking emergency special sessions (specifically a procedural vote in the Security Council that was not subject to the veto).[60] This procedure had been put in place in 1950, during the Korean War, by means of the Uniting for Peace Resolution adopted by a Western-dominated General Assembly. The content of the Uniting for Peace Resolution went much further than simply putting in place a procedure for transferring a situation when the Security Council was deadlocked, given that it purportedly claimed competence for the Assembly to recommend military enforcement measures in the cases of breaches of the peace and acts of aggression.[61]

Hugely controversial, Uniting for Peace has not been fully invoked by the General Assembly, although it can be argued that it has existing competence under Articles 10, 11 and 14 of the Charter, which grant the Assembly powers of recommendation in the area of peace and security. The argument that only the Security Council can authorise enforcement action under Chapter VII can be countered by reasoning that only the Security Council can order or require enforcement action, while the General Assembly is restricted to recommending such.[62]

---

59 *Certain Expenses of the United Nations*, (1962) ICJ Rep 151 at 164–5.
60 UNSC Res 119 (1956); UNSC Res 157 (1960).
61 UNGA Res 577 (1950).
62 *Expenses* case, *supra* note 59, at 163 – discussing the term 'action' in Art 11(2) of the UN Charter.

The prospect of the General Assembly recommending military action in the face of a veto or vetoes in the Security Council would in all likelihood generate a constitutional crisis in the UN but, arguably, without such a crisis there is little prospect of addressing the dreadful failures of the Security Council even to fulfil its basic diplomatic function, for example in Syria, where crimes against humanity and a threat to regional peace have subsisted since 2011.[63] If the General Assembly were to step in, and it has been increasingly critical of the Security Council's inaction over Syria,[64] it would not simply be a case of the UN's organ for justice trying to perform the role of the police.

The Assembly has a credible history of seeing security issues through the lens of injustice involving denials of human rights and self-determination.[65] For example, it was bitterly critical of the Security Council for not imposing wider mandatory sanctions on South Africa during the apartheid years, and recommended economic measures of its own.[66] Indeed, in its opinion on the legality of the construction of a security wall by Israel in the Palestinian occupied territories, the ICJ endorsed this competence. The General Assembly had adopted a resolution requesting an advisory opinion from the Court, in an emergency special session originally convoked under Uniting for Peace. The Court saw the construction of the wall, inter alia, as a denial of the Palestinian right to self-determination.[67]

On this basis the General Assembly should act in the instance of Syria, and it should have intervened in the instance of Kosovo in 1999, when the Security Council was unable to agree on how to prevent further crimes against humanity being committed by Serbian forces there. In that instance, NATO stepped into the breach and undertook a bombing campaign against Serbian forces, which eventually led to Serbian withdrawal from the province. This raises the issue of whether other security communities, such as NATO, have the competence to address threats to the peace when the UN is unable or unwilling to act.

---

63 Human Rights Council, 'Report of the Independent International Commission of Inquiry on the Syrian Arab Republic', UN Doc A/HRC/S-17/2/Add.1 (2011).

64 UNGA Res 66/253 (2011).

65 White, *supra* note 22, 169–72.

66 Terminated by UNGA Res 48/1 (1993).

67 *Legal Consequences of the Construction of a Wall in the Occupied Palestinian Territory*, (2004) ICJ Rep paras 24–35.

It is legitimate for a regional organisation to take military action to address major threats presented by genocide or crimes against humanity being committed within one of its member states, if the member states have agreed to that in the constitutive act setting up the regional organisation, and the UN is unable or unwilling to take action.[68] Such claims have yet to be fully tested against Article 53 of the UN Charter, which states that any regional enforcement action requires the authority of the UN Security Council, but if the Security Council is unable to act due to the veto or to inertia in the P5 then a legitimately constituted and empowered regional organisation has a strong claim to be able to step in within its region. Of course this does not permit NATO, a self-defence organisation, from taking non-defensive action outside its membership without any Security Council authorisation. In this regard the Kosovo action was not used as a precedent for intervention in Libya in 2011 – when crimes against humanity in Benghazi were about to be committed – when NATO states argued for and gained an authorisation from the Security Council for military action to protect civilians.[69] The issue of which organisations should shoulder the 'responsibility to protect' civilian populations under existential threat will be returned to in Chapter 8.

5.7   Conclusion

In the swirling stormy world of politics and law that is collective security, how do we draw a line between the two when laws appear so indeterminate? Formalist lawyers may well ask what is meant by 'enforcement', 'action', 'self-defence', 'concurring', 'measures necessary', 'threat to the peace', 'protection of civilians', 'collective', 'peace' and 'security' – just a few of the indeterminate words and terms that abound in this area. If we have no clarity as to the meaning of these terms, then any detailed rules or laws built upon them are equally suspect. In these circumstances it can be argued that, pragmatically, laws are entirely tools to be used to justify politics and power and, further, cannot be said to play a normative, determinative role. According to the pragmatic position, politics are not constrained by law; rather, law is entirely a product and consequence of politics.

---

68 Art 4 of the Constitutive Act of the African Union of 2000.
69 UNSC Res 1973 (2011).

But if it is accepted by all members of the P5 and, moreover, widely accepted in the UN membership that 'concurring' in the context of the voting rules of the Security Council in Article 27 effectively includes a permanent member abstaining on a substantive resolution; and that 'necessary measures' is UN-speak for military action, which requires a clear 'authorisation' from the Security Council, then we have a clear understanding of key legal terms. This means that any unilateral interpretations that depart from this consensus are likely to be self-interested legal justifications for political action that violate the shared understandings underpinning collective security.[70]

For instance in the build-up to the invasion of Iraq in 2003, the US and the UK failed to persuade the remaining members of the Security Council that the terms of Resolution 1441 of 2002, which spoke of 'serious consequences' for a 'material breach' of Iraq's disarmament obligations, were an authorisation to use force against Iraq. That might be the spin put on these terms by the US and the UK in an attempt to justify their actions domestically and internationally, but they were not the framework of terms and understandings of those terms that had been put in place to regulate the use of the most serious power at the Security Council's disposal – the power to authorise potentially devastating military force to tackle a threat to the peace. This means that law continues to play not just a consequential but also a constraining role in the area of collective security.

---

70 See I. Johnstone, 'Security Council Deliberations: The Power of Better Argument' (2003) 13 *EJIL* 437. More generally I. Johnstone, 'Treaty Interpretation: The Authority of Interpretive Communities' (1991) 12 *Michigan Journal of International Law* 371.

6 The law of armed conflict

6.1 Historical introduction

According to an eminent jurist, Hilaire McCoubrey, the law of armed conflict, also known as the *jus in bello* or international humanitarian law, 'seeks to moderate the conduct of armed conflict and mitigate the suffering which it causes'.[1] It is often divided loosely into two limbs: 'Hague' law following the Hague Conventions of 1899 and 1907 concerned with regulating the methods and means of warfare (the conduct of hostilities, tactics and weapons usage); and 'Geneva' law following the Geneva Conventions of 1949 and the two 1977 Additional Protocols to those Conventions, concerned with the protection of victims of armed conflicts (those who have become *hors de combat* – former combatants who are captured, injured, shipwrecked and non-combatant civilians).[2]

Although forms of the *jus in bello* can be traced back to antiquity, its modern form originated in the mid-nineteenth century by which time any trace of chivalry or moral fighting code had been lost, reaching its nadir in the Crimean War 1854–1855. Three years later, a Swiss businessman, Henry Dunant, after witnessing the carnage in the aftermath of the Battle of Solferino 1859, fought during the Franco–Austrian War, campaigned for the establishment of an International Red Cross Movement and the formulation of the first humanitarian Geneva Convention of 1864, which, unsurprisingly, was directed at improving the protection of wounded soldiers.

While the idea of having laws applicable to war, when normal conditions of law and order have broken down, may seem to be contradictory, Dunant was faced with the *unnecessary* suffering of those left to die of injuries on the battlefield. The point is that the law

---

1 H. McCoubrey, *International Humanitarian Law* (2nd edn, Aldershot: Ashgate, 1998) 1.
2 *Ibid.*, 2.

of armed conflict does not seek to silence the guns, it seeks to mitigate the effects of conflict. Sometimes this takes the form of preventing certain military tactics or weapons that might enable a quicker victory, such as explosive bullets (prohibited by the 1868 Declaration of St Petersburg initiated by Russia), but states can, subject to any such agreed limitations, use maximum force to achieve their military objectives. States agree to limitations from a combination of self-interest and reciprocity. For instance, although Russia had developed the explosive bullet in the 1860s, it realised that any military advantage that it might gain would be short-lived once other more industrialised countries, such as Britain, France or Germany, produced them in greater quantities.[3]

Furthermore, the law tended to be a reaction to new developments in a broader sense, so that, although the protection of wounded was reasonably effective amidst the catastrophic losses of the First World War,[4] the development of submarine warfare in that conflict, and the mistreatment of civilians during the Second World War, led to further treaties so that when the law was consolidated and developed in 1949 four detailed treaties were necessary: the First Geneva Convention on Wounded and Sick in the Field 1949, the Second Geneva Convention on Wounded and Sick at Sea 1949, the Third Geneva Convention on Prisoners of War 1949, and the Fourth Geneva Convention on Protection of Civilians 1949. The law relating to inter-state conflicts, was enhanced even further by the adoption of Additional Protocol I in 1977.

The law of armed conflict was developed in the context of war between states. Until comparatively recently, it applied only to conflicts of an international nature and had no application to internal conflicts, such as civil wars and rebellions. The only exceptions occurred in the case of large-scale civil wars in which the participants were internationally recognised as having belligerent status and thus regarded by the international community as engaging in war (the classic examples are the American Civil War and the Spanish Civil War).[5]

---

3 *Ibid.*, 19.

4 See now Arts 12–22 GC III 1949; Art 11 AP I 1977. The abbreviations GC I, GC II, GC III and GC IV will be used in the footnotes to refer to the four Geneva Conventions of 1949; while the abbreviations AP I and AP II refer to the 1977 Protocols.

5 UK Ministry of Defence, *The Manual of the Law of Armed Conflict* (Oxford University Press, 2004) 27.

The development of any law of armed conflict for non-international wars was restricted by the idea that a sovereign state had an untrammelled right to deal with any rebellion or challenge to its monopoly over the use of force – meaning that rebels were seen as criminals not legitimate combatants. This objection retains some of its force despite the development of increasingly detailed sets of principles and rules governing internal conflicts, first in Common Article 3 found in all four of the above-mentioned Geneva Conventions of 1949, then Additional Protocol II of 1977, and arguably, even further, by a combination of international criminal tribunals, principally the International Criminal Tribunal for the Former Yugoslavia (ICTY), and customary international law.

The law of armed conflict is replete with rules. An examination of the Geneva Conventions shows that armed conflict seems to be one of the most regulated areas of human activity, which is encouraging on the one hand, but on the other seems to fly in the face of the evidence where conflicts as bloody as the Battle of Solferino still occur with appalling regularity. Although these bloody conflicts are mainly of an internal nature – in Sri Lanka, Democratic Republic of Congo (DRC), and Syria in the twenty-first century, as examples – the failure of international society and international law to curtail violations of the basic principles underlying the law of armed conflict requires examination and understanding.

6.2   Reciprocity

Has the point been reached where the gap between law and practice is so vast that the law is no longer valid and requires a total restructuring? This might, for example, take the form of a move away from reciprocity, which may still work for inter-state conflict, towards centralised enforcement against governments and non-state actors who ignore basic principles in their fratricidal internal or existential transnational struggles. Reciprocity could be said to be the key underlying principle upon which the law governing war was built. It is premised on each state to a conflict sticking to the rules so that if, for example, one state mistreats prisoners of war (PoWs) then so might the other. The result is that generally both states treat their PoWs in accordance with the Third Geneva Convention of 1949.

There are detailed rules in the Third Geneva Convention on PoWs relating to their humane treatment,[6] and include, for example, the well-known rule that a PoW only has to give his or her name, rank, date of birth and serial number when questioned.[7] While these rules have the benefit of relative simplicity as well as clarity, there remain difficult problems about who is entitled to PoW status. The rules in the Geneva Convention are not without problems in interpretation but it appears that there are three types of combatants entitled to PoW status upon their capture or surrender: those belonging to the regular armed forces, others not in uniform but carrying arms openly and bearing some distinguishing sign visible at a distance, and then others who are precluded from wearing such signs but are still carrying their arms openly.[8]

The somewhat old-fashioned notion is that the normal combatant is a soldier in uniform, the embodiment of a state agent, clearly distinguishing him or her from the enemy and clearly distinguishing him or her from civilians. Such a perception is increasingly untenable, even sometimes in international armed conflicts between states – for example between US/UK forces and the Taliban regime in Afghanistan in 2001, where the Taliban were seen, initially at least, as not meeting the criteria of combatants, but neither did a number of the special forces deployed by the US and the UK.

The status of unlawful combatants – fighters not granted a privileged status when captured – given to prisoners captured by the US in the 'war on terror' and held in detention centres such as Guantanamo Bay, is one not clearly recognised by the Geneva Conventions. This uneven treatment of prisoners reflects the erosion of reciprocity in modern warfare,[9] although the US relied on the US Supreme Court's decision of 1944 (*Ex parte Quirin*), where Nazi saboteurs out of uniform were caught in the US in 1942 and were not given PoW status upon capture. The Supreme Court agreed that the laws of war drew a distinction between lawful and unlawful combatants – 'lawful combatants are subject to capture and detention as prisoners of war by opposing military forces. Unlawful combatants are likewise subject

---

6 Arts 13–16 GC III 1949.

7 Art 17 GC III 1949.

8 Art 4 GC III 1949; Art 44(3) AP I 1977.

9 J.D. Ohlin, 'Is the Jus in Bello in Crisis?' (2013) 11 *Journal of International Criminal Justice* 27 at 29.

to capture and detention, but in addition they are subject to trial and punishment by military tribunals for acts which render their belligerency unlawful'.[10] Emily Crawford doubts the precedential value of a domestic case decided before the advent of the Geneva Conventions.[11] Furthermore, the flawed military commissions established by the US to try some of the Guantanamo detainees have also been subject to heavy criticism.[12]

However, when it comes to internal and other non-international armed conflicts then there are no requirements to treat captured combatants as PoWs, only a general exhortation to both sides in Common Article 3 to 'treat humanely' 'persons taking no active part in hostilities, including members of armed forces who have laid down their arms and those placed hors de combat by sickness, wounds, detention ...'; and more specific prohibitions on 'violence to life and person', the 'taking of hostages', 'outrages upon personal dignity', and 'the passing of sentences and the carrying out of executions without previous judgment pronounced by a regularly constituted court, affording all judicial guarantees which are recognized as indispensable by civilized peoples'.[13] The latter should now be interpreted in the light of requirements on state parties from human rights treaties, which will apply during internal armed conflicts unless derogated from.

Following from this, it could be argued that in internal armed conflicts potentially the greater protection for civilians and those rebels captured by government forces comes from the human rights obligations placed on states, rather than the rules of international humanitarian law based on reciprocity, which is not inherently present in internal conflicts. Nonetheless, this does not provide a ready solution as evidence also shows that the enforcement of human rights law in internal conflicts is weak, dependent upon pressure from civil society and NGOs, and upon naming and shaming techniques, for example, before the Human Rights Committee reviewing states' reports under the International

---

10 *Ex parte Quirin et al* (1942) 317 U.S. 1 at 30–31.

11 E. Crawford, *The Treatment of Combatants and Insurgents under the Law of Armed Conflict* (Oxford University Press, 2010) 60.

12 H. Duffy, *The 'War on Terror' and the Framework of International Law* (Cambridge University Press, 2005) 379–442.

13 See also Arts 5 and 6 AP II 1977. The US Supreme Court has used Article 75 AP I 1977 (which includes more detail on fair trial guarantees) to interpret Common article 3 – *Hamdam v Rumsfeld*, 126 S. Ct. 2749 (2006).

Covenant on Civil and Political Rights or receiving individual complaints under the Optional Protocol. Although it has been argued that
it is possible for non-state actors to have human rights obligations,[14]
the evidence of the acceptance of this is limited. Thus, human rights
obligations in an internal conflict fall primarily on the government side
and not on the rebels.

The principle of reciprocity under the law of armed conflict works
when two states clash and it is in their own self-interest to uphold
the laws of war, which are equally binding on both parties irrespective of the causes of war. There is sufficient balance between the parties to deliver reciprocal protection. However, asymmetrical conflicts
between a state with a developed military and a state which relies
on militias and irregular fighters, or between a developed state and a
transnational terrorist group, or between a government and armed
groups in an internal conflict (but maybe with transnational elements)
do not by themselves create these conditions. Paradigmatically, in the
latter instance, the government is reluctant to recognise that insurgent
groups have any status or rights to the extent of denying that any
armed conflict exists, and both the government and insurgents are
often involved in existential struggles, the aim of which is to eliminate
the other, not just to achieve victory. The aim in such conflicts is not
to establish a strong position on which to negotiate a peace (though
this may happen when mutual exhaustion prevails or outside support
is removed), but to keep or change the status quo; to retain an existing (or to create a new) legal and political order. It remains possible
that the government might take the lead and start treating captured
insurgents as PoWs in the hope that this might encourage reciprocal
treatment of captured government soldiers by the insurgents,[15] or vice
versa or, indeed, both parties may declare themselves committed to
such principles, but given the nature of internecine struggles this will
be very much the exception rather than the rule.[16]

The author of the Lieber Code of 1863, developed in the context of
the American Civil War, but widely influential on later developments
in the laws of war, described the nature of guerrilla operations as
consisting of:

---

14 Crawford, *supra* note 11, 126–9.

15 *Ibid.*, 158.

16 But see S. Sivakumaran, 'Binding Armed Opposition Groups' (2006) 55 *ICLQ* 369.

self-constituted sets of armed men in times of war, who form no integrant part of the organized army, do not stand on the regular payroll of the army, or are not paid at all, take up arms and lay them down at intervals, and carry on petty war (guerrilla) chiefly by raids, extortion, destruction, and massacre, and who cannot encumber themselves with many prisoners, and will generally give no quarter.[17]

This description of warfare between irregulars on both sides, taking no prisoners and giving no quarter,[18] remains accurate when considering the conflicts mentioned and others besides.

The highpoint in a movement towards treating insurgents as having combatant status (and therefore being entitled to kill and not to be prosecuted except for war crimes) was the controversial recognition of national liberation movements in Article 1(4) of Additional Protocol I of 1977, which stated that international armed conflicts (to which the whole of the 1949 Conventions and Additional Protocol I apply) included 'armed conflicts in which peoples are fighting against colonial domination and alien occupation and against racist regimes in the exercise of their right of self-determination . . .'. Rather than clarifying the position of insurgencies this has led to often futile claims that this principle should apply to certain armed struggles (but not others). What is clear is that this provision was not intended to cover every internal fight for 'freedom', but is limited to colonial or related struggles for independence.[19]

6.3   Distinction

The law of armed conflict is premised upon there being a distinction between combatants and other legitimate military targets on the one

---

17 F. Lieber, 'Guerrilla Parties Considered with Reference to the Laws and Usages if War' in Hartigan, *Lieber's Code and the Law* (Chicago: Precedent Publishing, 1983) 41. See further D. Kritsiotis, 'International Law and the Violence of Non-State Actors' in K.H. Kaikobad and M. Bohlander (eds), *International Law and Power: Perspectives on Legal Order and Justice* (Leiden: Martinus Nijhoff, 2009) 343.

18 'No Quarter' – orders that there should be no survivors – are prohibited by Art 40 AP I 1977. On origins see McCoubrey, *supra* note 1, 217.

19 See generally N. Higgins, *Regulating the Use of Force in Wars of National Liberation: The Need for a New Regime: A Study of the South Moluccas and Aceh* (Leiden: Martinus Nijhoff, 2010).

hand, and civilians and civilian targets on the other.[20] The problem is that in modern conflicts, whether internal or international, there is considerable cross-over from civilians to combatants – where an individual may be a civilian by day and a guerrilla by night. In 2009 the ICRC tried to update the law by giving the following guidance on when civilians should be considered as taking part in hostilities (and therefore losing their protected status). The guidance states that:

> For the purposes of the principle of distinction in international armed conflict, all persons who are neither members of the armed forces of a party to the conflict nor participants in a levee en masse are civilians and, therefore, entitled to protection against direct attack unless and for such time as they take a direct part in hostilities.[21]

And in relation to non-international armed conflicts the ICRC guidance states:

> For the purposes of the principle of distinction in non-international armed conflict, all persons who are not members of the State armed forces or organized armed groups of a party to the conflict are civilians and, therefore, entitled to protection against direct attack unless and for such time as they take a direct part in hostilities. In non-international armed conflict, organized armed groups constitute the armed forces of a non-State party to the conflict and consist only of individuals whose continuous function is to take a direct part in hostilities ('continuous combat function').[22]

This constitutes a valid and necessary attempt to update the principle of distinction, although the introduction of 'continuous combat

---

20 See for example Art 48 AP I 1977 which states that '. . . the Parties to the conflict shall at all times distinguish between the civilian population and combatants and between civilian objects and military objectives and accordingly shall direct their operations only against military objectives'. See also detailed rules in Arts 52–6 AP I 1977. For non-international armed conflicts see Arts 13–18 AP II 1977.

21 ICRC, 'Interpretive Guidance on the Notion of Direct Participation in Hostilities under International Humanitarian Law', adopted by the ICRC Assembly on 26 February 2009, Recommendation I. A 'levee en masse' consists of 'inhabitants of non-occupied territory, who on the approach of the enemy, spontaneously take up arms to resist the invading force, without having had time to form themselves into regular armed units, provided they carry arms openly and respect the laws and customs of war' – Art 4 GC III 1949.

22 ICRC, 'Interpretive Guidance on the Notion of Direct Participation in Hostilities under International Humanitarian Law', *supra* note 21, Recommendation II.

function' does not necessarily meet the objections to modern warfare first identified by Francis Lieber above, where insurgents will generally deliberately operate in the zone between civilians who may occasionally participate in hostilities (for example when defending family or group) and full time rebel soldiers.

Such issues came to the fore in the killing of Osama bin Laden on 2 May 2011 by US special forces in a compound in a largely peaceful town in Pakistan. The law as stated would suggest that bin Laden had (regained) civilian status at the time of his killing, in that he was neither a direct participant in hostilities nor belonging to a non-state party to a conflict in Pakistan undertaking a continuous combat function. However, as the leader of al-Qaeda, an organisation engaged in a continuous combat function although not in the area of Pakistan in which bin Laden was killed, he arguably was a legitimate military target in a non-international armed conflict between the US and al-Qaeda. This was certainly the position of the US in justifying its action: 'in this ongoing armed conflict, the United States has the authority under international law . . . to use force, including lethal force, to defend itself, including by targeting persons such as high-level al-Qaeda leaders who are planning attacks . . .'. Such 'individuals who are part of such an armed group are belligerents and, therefore, lawful targets under international law'; and furthermore a 'state that is engaged in an armed conflict or in legitimate self-defense is not required to provide targets with legal process before the state may use lethal force'. 'Finally, consistent with the laws of armed conflict . . . the US forces were prepared to capture bin Laden if he had surrendered in a way that they could safely accept', although there was no 'genuine offer of surrender' by bin Laden.[23] If the law of war paradigm was applicable, as the US argued, this was a lawful killing; but, if this was deemed to be outside any armed conflict then a law enforcement paradigm was applicable where lethal force, under accepted human rights standards, is only justifiable in self-defence, defence of third parties, or when absolutely necessary to prevent escape.[24]

23 H.H. Koh, Legal Adviser to the State Department, 'The Lawfulness of the U.S. Operation Against Osama bin Laden', *Opinio Juris*, 19 May, 2011, at http://opiniojuris.org/2011/05/19/the-lawfulness-of-the-us-operation-against-osama-bin-laden/.

24 L. Doswald Beck, *Human Rights in Times of Conflict and Terrorism* (Oxford University Press, 2011) 161–3.

Targeting also raises problems of distinction. The basic rule is that only military objectives may be attacked.[25] According to Additional Protocol I of 1977, 'military objectives are limited to those objects which by their nature, location, purpose or use make an effective contribution to military action and whose total or partial destruction, capture or neutralization, in the circumstances ruling at the time, offers a definite military advantage'.[26] This leaves plenty of scope for interpretation and lists have been made including within them soldiers, tanks, roads and bridges.[27] However, while soldiers and tanks are inherently legitimate targets, roads and bridges can only be legitimate targets if they are making a contribution to military action and their destruction must offer a definite military advantage.

These issues have not disappeared with the advent of more surgical and accurate means and methods of warfare. In fact, in a number of recent conflicts the desire by militarily advanced states to conduct 'zero casualty warfare', for instance by aerial bombing in Kosovo 1999 and Libya 2011, or by using unmanned drones in Afghanistan/Pakistan and elsewhere,[28] has resulted in a number of problematic targeting decisions. Furthermore, there are limited or no casualties on one side of the conflict only, again challenging the reciprocal basis of the laws of war. If one state is being hit by surgical strikes against legitimate targets but has no capacity to hit back at the military of the attacking state, it might be tempted into unlawful acts, for example by taking foreign national hostages or by using them as military shields.

Under the rules of international humanitarian law the firing of missiles from drones at military targets is lawful even if it leads to 'collateral damage', which is defined as 'incidental loss of civilian life, injury to civilians, damage to civilian objects, or a combination thereof',[29] but any response that purports to hide possible military targets behind civilians or situate them in intensely populated areas is unjustified.[30]

---

25 Art 52(1) AP I 1977. See generally W. Boothby, 'Does the Law of Targeting Meet 21st Century Needs?' in C. Harvey, J. Summers and N.D. White (eds), *Contemporary Challenges to the Laws of War: Essays in Honour of Peter Rowe* (Cambridge University Press, 2014).
26 Art 52(2) AP I 1977.
27 A.P.V. Rogers, *Law on the Battlefield* (2nd edn, Manchester University Press, 2004) 83–5.
28 On drones see D. Turns, 'Droning On: Some International Humanitarian Law Aspects of the Use of Unmanned Aerial Vehicles in Contemporary Conflicts' in Harvey, Summers and White, *supra* note 25.
29 Art 51(5)(b) AP I 1977.
30 Art 51(7) AP I 1977.

While that is the clear legal position, the conditions of unevenness in military capabilities between the parties to the conflict, whether between militarily advanced nations and developing countries, or between heavily armed and supplied government forces and poorly or lesser armed rebels, destroys the reciprocal basis of application of the laws of war, pushing the weaker side into unlawful acts that, in turn, may lead the stronger side into widening its list of targets – so-called 'target creep' – particularly when it has hit all the obvious targets.

Two controversial targeting decisions made by NATO during the Kosovo Conflict of 1999, when NATO operations were conducted entirely by aerial means, serve to illustrate the problems faced by commanders in applying the law. The targeting of the bridge on Grdelica Gorge on 12 April 1999, when a train carrying civilians was crossing the bridge, was justified because the bridge and railway were part of Serbia's supply network. In a report prepared by the ICTY Prosecutor's Committee it was determined that the bridge was a legitimate target although the train was not. Since it was the bridge that was targeted by NATO, not the train, the attack was lawful.[31] If indeed this is the clear legal position, the legitimacy of the strike must be doubted given the presence of the train.

More controversially, on 23 April 1999 NATO attacked the Serbian TV and Radio Station (RTS), causing loss of life, justifying its strike on the basis of the dual use of the station for military communications as well as civilian broadcasting, although this was overshadowed by its claim that RTS was inciting crimes by Serbian forces and broadcasting propaganda. If the latter was truly the main reason then the strike could not really deliver a definite military advantage and was therefore unlawful.[32]

---

31 Final Report to the Prosecutor by the Committee Established to Review the NATO Bombing Campaign Against the Federal Republic of Yugoslavia, para 62. See also the Committee's discussion of NATO's attack on the Djakovica convoy on 14 April 1999 when civilian tractors and other vehicles were destroyed with loss of life. The Committee decided that there was insufficient recklessness for war crimes charges (*Ibid.*, para 70).

32 G. Aldrich, 'Yugoslavia's Television Studios as Military Objectives' (1999) 1 *International Law Forum* 149–50.

6.4   Humanity

In many ways the *raison d'être* of international *humanitarian* law is its insistence on humanity in warfare, commencing in the modern era with Henri Dunant's witnessing of the suffering of the wounded after the Battle of Solferino. The principle of humanity is embodied in the Martens Clause located in the preamble to Hague Convention IV of 1907,[33] which provided that 'in cases not included in the Regulations . . . inhabitants and . . . belligerents remain under the protection of the rules and principles of the law of nations, as they result from the usages established among civilised peoples, from the laws of humanity, and the dictates of public conscience'.[34] According to the UK Manual of the Law of Armed Conflict 'humanity forbids the infliction of suffering, injury, or destruction not actually necessary for the accomplishment of legitimate purposes'.[35]

International humanitarian law is at its most developed in its protection of the wounded, at least in relation to international armed conflict.[36] Provisions include the requirement that all possible measures be taken to search for and collect the wounded and sick,[37] and any prioritisation in treatment must be by medical need,[38] which must be in accordance with 'generally accepted medical standards'.[39] There are similar duties imposed by the Second Geneva Convention 1949 in relation to wounded, sick and shipwrecked at sea. These include the positive duty to search and rescue survivors,[40] which does not oblige the commander of the searching vessel to risk his or her ship. This was the reason given as to why the British submarine – HMS *Conqueror* – did not attempt rescue of Argentinian sailors shipwrecked by the *Conqueror*'s torpedo attack on the Argentinian cruiser *General Belgrano* during the Falklands conflict of 1982. In relation to non-international armed conflicts the rules for protection of wounded are, as with many aspects of the law of armed conflict, less developed.[41]

---

33   On the origins of the Martens clause see Rogers, *supra* note 27, 7.

34   See also Art 1(2) AP I 1977; and the Preamble AP II 1977.

35   UK, *Manual of the Law of Armed Conflict, supra* note 5, 23.

36   Art 12 GC I 1949.

37   Art 15 GC I 1949.

38   Art 12 GC I 1949.

39   Art 11 AP I 1977.

40   Art 18 GC II 1949.

41   Common Article 3(2); Arts 7–10 AP II 1977.

6.5   Military necessity

The laws of humanity and the dictates of public conscience are qualified by military necessity. This has already been seen in the rules that allow for incidental civilian losses and those that can be interpreted as allowing commanders of submarines not to expose themselves unnecessarily to attack by surfacing to rescue survivors. When looking overall at the purposes of armed conflict law, the UK Manual of the Law of Armed Conflict states that 'it is intended to minimize the suffering caused by armed conflict rather than impede military efficiency'.[42]

However, the point has been made that military necessity does not override the rules of international humanitarian law, rather it is confined by that law, which takes account of other principles such as humanity, distinction and proportionality.[43] This was recognised in one of the early modern expositions of the law, the Lieber Code of 1863, which defined military necessity as 'those measures which are indispensable to securing the ends of the war and which are lawful according to the modern law and usages of war' (Article 14).

The Regulations Respecting the Laws and Customs of War on Land annexed to the Fourth Hague Convention of 1907 made it clear that the 'right of belligerents to adopt means of injuring the enemy is not unlimited', and specifically forbade poisoned weapons and the employment of arms, projectiles or material calculated to cause unnecessary suffering (Articles 22 and 23). Similar rules are found in Additional Protocol I of 1977, adding also the prohibition of methods or means of warfare that are intended or expected 'to cause widespread, long-term and severe damage to the natural environment'.[44] The Protocol also imposed a duty on state parties to determine whether new weapons would be prohibited under the Protocol or other relevant rules of international law.[45]

The question is whether these rules, which again depend upon reciprocity to induce compliance by states, are strong enough to prevent the development of weapons that cause unnecessary suffering of combatants and those civilians that may be 'incidentally' affected. White

---

42 UK, *Manual of the Law of Armed Conflict, supra* note 5, 21.

43 *Ibid.,* 23.

44 Art 35 AP I 1977.

45 Art 36 AP I 1977.

phosphorus is an example of a weapon developed and deployed by Israel in Gaza in 2008–2009 and the US in Fallujah (Iraq) in 2004 in order to create a fog of war behind which troops could advance. However, its burning effects on individuals caught under it led, in part, to the following conclusions in the Goldstone Report into Gaza of 2009.

> The Mission finds that in a number of cases Israel failed to take feasible precautions required by customary law reflected in article 57(2)(a)(ii) of Additional Protocol I to avoid or minimize incidental loss of civilian life, injury to civilians and damage to civilian objects. The firing of white phosphorus shells over the UNRWA compound in Gaza City is one of such cases in which precautions were not taken in the choice of weapons and methods in the attack, and these facts were compounded by reckless disregard for the consequences. The intentional strike at al-Quds hospital using high-explosive artillery shells and white phosphorous in and around the hospital also violated articles 18 and 19 of the Fourth Geneva Convention. With regard to the attack against al-Wafa hospital, the Mission found a violation of the same provisions, as well as a violation of the customary law prohibition against attacks which may be expected to cause excessive damage to civilians and civilian objects.[46]

6.6   Proportionality

According to the UK Manual of the Law of Armed Conflict the 'principle of proportionality is a link between the principles of military necessity and humanity. It is most evident in connection with the reduction of incidental damage caused by military operations'.[47] Included in the prohibition of indiscriminate attacks in Additional Protocol I, in other words, those that do not discriminate between military and civilian objectives,[48] are attacks which 'may be expected to cause incidental loss of civilian life, injury to civilians, damage to civilian objects, or a combination thereof, which would be excessive in relation to the concrete and direct military advantage anticipated'.[49]

---

46 Report of the UN Fact-Finding Mission on the Gaza Conflict, UN Doc A/HRC/12/48 (2009) para 1919.

47 UK, *Manual of the Law of Armed Conflict, supra* note 5, 25.

48 Art 51(4) AP I 1977.

49 Art 51(5)(b) AP I 1977.

Although these rules would clearly prohibit the sort of area bombing that the Allies launched against German cities such as Dresden
towards the end of the Second World War (which was arguably
unlawful at the time) since they are inherently indiscriminate and
disproportionate,[50] they would not rule out the more precise destruction of a munitions factory killing civilian workers and probably killing
or injuring many civilians living in the surrounding area if the military
advantages were deemed, by a reasonable commander, to outweigh
the civilian losses.[51]

The absence of objective standards that could be applied to this balanc-
ing act is evident on a massive scale in the debates about whether the
use of nuclear weapons by the US against Hiroshima and Nagasaki in
Japan in 1945, which brought an earlier end to the war and saved significant losses to US and Japanese forces, but at a massive cost in terms
of loss of civilian lives and poisoning of the environment. It seems
perverse, however, to balance the lives of civilians who are meant to
be protected against those of soldiers who are not (at least while they
remain as combatants). Given that indiscriminate attacks on civilians
are prohibited it should not be permissible to point to the military
advantages of the effects of undermining the overall war effort of the
enemy by the use of such devastating attacks.

Although the use of nuclear weapons is not, unlike chemical weapons,
specifically prohibited by international law, the indiscriminate effects
of such weapons signifies that their use is unlawful. Although the ICJ,
in its *Nuclear Weapons* opinion of 1996, ultimately remained equivo-
cal on the legality of nuclear weapons in the extreme circumstance
of when the 'very survival of the state was at stake', it did state that
normally the 'threat or use of nuclear weapons would generally be
contrary to the rules of international law applicable in armed conflict,
and in particular the principles and rules of humanitarian law'.[52] In the
end game of trying to ensure the survival of the state by using nuclear
weapons, states may well have stepped into the Hartian suicide club,
where international law has ceased to be relevant, although it is curious
that the ICJ, as the ultimate guardian of international law, recognised
this.

---

50 See specifically Art 51(5)(a) AP I 1977.
51 UK, *Manual of the Law of Armed Conflict*, *supra* note 5, 25.
52 *Legality of the Threat or Use of Nuclear Weapons*, (1996) ICJ Rep, para 105.

6.7   Protection of the environment

As a relative latecomer to the pantheon of principles underpinning the law of armed conflict protection of the environment during armed conflict is of growing concern. However, the established rules are directed at the protection of the population dependent upon the environment, rather than the environment per se. This is reflected in Additional Protocol I of 1977 where it is stated that:

> Care shall be taken in warfare to protect the environment against widespread, long-term and severe damage. This protection includes a prohibition of the use of methods or means of warfare which are intended or may be expected to cause such damage to the natural environment and thereby to prejudice the health or survival of the population.[53]

Furthermore, the level of envisaged damage to the environment is high and is certainly a long way from the precautionary principle that normally applies in environmental law.[54]

The use of defoliants such as Agents Blue and Orange by the US during the Vietnam War, and attempts at 'cloud seeding' during that conflict, which finished in 1975,[55] led to the UN Convention on the Prohibition of Military or any other Hostile Use of Environmental Modification Techniques of 1976, which prohibited 'any technique for changing – through the deliberate manipulation of natural processes – the dynamics, composition or structure of the Earth, including its biota, lithosphere, hydrosphere and atmosphere, or of outer space' (Article 2). Unfortunately, while this may be a useful standard in the future when weather/climate manipulation might be more effective, this does not cover the abuse of the environment that has occurred in recent armed conflicts, such as the burning of Kuwaiti oilfields by the Iraqi army in the face of its imminent defeat in Kuwait in 1991.[56]

---

53 Art 55 AP I 1977.

54 See Principle 15 of the Rio Declaration on Environment and Development 1992 (UN Doc A/ CONF.151/26): 'In order to protect the environment, the precautionary approach shall be widely applied by States according to their capabilities. Where there are threats of serious or irreversible damage, lack of full scientific certainty shall not be used as a reason for postponing cost-effective measures to prevent environmental degradation'.

55 McCoubrey, *supra* note 1, 227–9.

56 *Ibid.*, 330.

6.8   The existence and type of armed conflict

Much of the discussion above is premised on the continuing validity of the distinction between international and non-international armed conflicts. The protections provided in the former are still greater than those provided for in the latter. The reason is not one of logic but of history, where states have seen greater benefit in ensuring reciprocal obligations in international conflicts than having their hands tied in dealing with internal rebellions. States, after all, make international law.

In the nineteenth century, once a state of war existed between states the law of peace was replaced by the law of war, which contained:

> Rules primarily concerned with the rights and obligations of belligerents concerning their subjects, armies and property, and gradually started including some rudimentary rules on the means of warfare. The outbreak of war also triggered the laws of neutrality that governed the relations between the belligerents and third states. These special rights and obligations came into effect once the outbreak of war was notified or otherwise made known to the neutral states and expired with the cessation of the war. The laws of neutrality were thus designed to preserve the relations of third states with the belligerents as far as the circumstances allowed it.[57]

'War' was a legal concept that ultimately failed to fulfil its purpose (of establishing a clear legal regime to govern hostilities) since it was possible that there were full-scale hostilities between two states but no state of war existed because neither state recognised a state of war, or a war might be declared by both states but no fighting ensued. Thus, war as a legal concept gave way to a factual test threshold ('armed conflict') and the collapse of the formal distinction between law of war and law of peace. Nowadays the legal regimes overlap, with it being recognised that human rights law, for instance, continues to apply during armed conflict,[58] though the precise relationship between the *lex specialis* governing warfare (the law of armed conflict), and the *lex generalis*

---

57 M. Milanovic and V. Hadzi-Vidanovic, 'A Taxonomy of Armed Conflict' in N.D. White and C. Henderson (eds), *Research Handbook on International Conflict and Security Law* (Cheltenham: Edward Elgar Publishing, 2013) 256 at 259.

58 As recognised by the International Court in its advisory opinions on *Legality of the Threat or Use of Nuclear Weapons*, (1996) ICJ Rep para 25; and *Legal Consequences of the Construction of a Wall in the Occupied Palestinian Territory*, (2004) ICJ Rep paras 102–6.

applying during war and peace is evolving.[59] One area of relative clarity is in the area of the right to life, where the normal restrictions on the use of lethal force, contained in human rights law, give way to those rules that allow for combatants to use lethal force within the confines of international humanitarian law during armed conflict.[60]

Although the trigger of 'armed conflict' is a great improvement on 'war', there is, unfortunately, no definition of 'armed conflict' in the Conventions or Protocols. The most utilised definition, covering both international (between states) and non-international (between a state and an armed group or between armed groups) was given only relatively recently by the ICTY in the *Tadic* case: 'An armed conflict exists whenever there is a resort to armed force between States or protracted armed violence between governmental authorities and organised armed groups or between such groups within a State'.[61]

This would suggest that any use of force between states would trigger the law of armed conflict, while for an armed conflict to exist within a state or between a state and a non-state actor then there must be 'protracted armed violence'. For instance, in Syria the ICRC only declared that an 'armed conflict' existed between the government and armed groups in July 2012, when violence had started in March 2011.

According to Additional Protocol II of 1977 'situations of internal disturbances and tensions, such as riots, isolated and sporadic acts of violence and other acts of similar nature' do not amount to 'armed conflicts',[62] meaning that the law of armed conflict does not apply, though human rights law and aspects of international criminal law remain applicable. Often a government will categorise extensive internal violence as something less than armed conflict in order to avoid admitting it has lost control or give credence to a rebellion. For instance, France treated the Algerian insurgency as an internal disturbance in the period 1954–1956; and the UK dealt with the 'troubles' in Northern Ireland from the late 1960s as an internal disturbance.

---

59 I. Scobbie, 'Principle or Pragmatics? The Relationship between Human Rights Law and the Law of Armed Conflict' (2009) 14 *JCSL* 449; M. Milanovic, 'A Norm Conflict Perspective on the Relationship between International Humanitarian Law and Human Rights Law' (2009) 14 *JCSL* 459.

60 C. Garraway, 'To Kill or Not to Kill? Dilemmas on the Use of Force', (2009) 14 *JCSL* 499.

61 *Prosecutor v Tadic* (1996) 105 ILR 419 at 488.

62 Art 1(2) AP II 1977.

Somewhat paradoxically, Additional Protocol II of 1977 establishes a threshold for conflict that is higher than that stated in the *Tadic* case, requiring the existence of an armed conflict taking place 'in the territory of a High Contracting Party between its armed forces and dissident armed forces or other armed groups which, under responsible command, exercise such control over a part of its territory as to enable them to carry out sustained and concerted military operations and to implement this Protocol'.[63]

It is the category of non-international armed conflicts that, while arguably the most important in this day and age, is the most difficult and problematic. Historically it relates to internal conflicts, but has been applied, by the US Supreme Court, for example, to transnational conflicts between states and non-state actors (such as international terrorist groups).[64] On the other hand, the Israeli Supreme Court decided that the transnational nature of such terrorist conflicts meant that they should be viewed as international for the purposes of international humanitarian law.[65] Thus, there is a lack of clarity as international humanitarian law struggles to keep pace with modern conflicts.[66]

In relation to internal conflicts a useful summary of the applicable law is provided by the UK Manual of the Law of Armed Conflict:

> The application of the law of armed conflict to internal hostilities thus depends upon a number of factors. In the first place, it does not apply at all unless an armed conflict exists. If an armed conflict exists, the provisions of Common Article 3 apply. Should the dissidents achieve a degree of success and exercise the necessary control over a part of the territory, the provisions of Additional Protocol II come into force. Finally, if the conflict is recognized as a conflict falling within Additional Protocol I, Article 1(4), it becomes subject to the Geneva Conventions and Protocol I.[67]

---

63 Art 1(1) AP II 1977.
64 *Hamdam v Rumsfeld, supra* note 13.
65 *The Public Committee against Torture in Israel v Government of Israel* HCJ 769/02, 13 December 2006.
66 For useful discussion, see L. Moir, 'It's a Bird! It's a Plane! It's a Non-International Armed Conflict: Cross Border Hostilities Between States and Non-State Actors' in Harvey, Summers and White (eds), *supra* note 25.
67 UK, *Manual of the Law of Armed Conflict, supra* note 5, 33.

As has already been stated Common Article 3 of the Geneva Conventions of 1949 applies 'in the case of armed conflicts not of an international character occurring in the territory of' a state. It is also argued that customary law provides a greater level of protection,[68] but it does not, for instance, provide for PoW status and, although civilians should be safeguarded, issues such as collateral damage are much more opaque in internal conflicts where rebel factions will often not distinguish themselves sufficiently from the civilian population.

The complexity of armed conflict does not end there for it is entirely feasible than hostilities will actually involve a mixture of conflicts. Such 'mixed conflicts' were recognised in the *Tadic* case:

> It is indisputable that an armed conflict is international if it takes place between two or more States. In addition, in a case of an internal armed conflict breaking out on the territory of a State, it may become international (or, depending upon the circumstances, be international in character alongside an internal armed conflict) if (i) another State intervenes in that conflict through its troops or alternatively if (ii) some of the participants in the internal armed conflict act on behalf of that other State.[69]

It follows that the initial conflict in Afghanistan in 2001 was mixed – an internal conflict between the Taliban government and Northern Alliance rebels, and international between US/UK forces and the Taliban, and further, arguably, non-international between the US and al-Qaeda. With the defeat of the Taliban, the conflict between ISAF (a NATO-led force acting under the authority of the Security Council) and the Taliban became non-international as the Taliban are the insurgents and ISAF forces are there with the agreement of the government and in a supporting role.[70] The conflict in Libya in 2011 was also mixed – internal between the rebels and the government of Gaddafi, and international between the government and NATO.[71] While seemingly unduly complex, the central problem remains not one of which a set of rules apply but compliance (or lack of such) by at least one of the parties in modern conflicts.

---

68 For authoritative analysis of the customary rules applicable in both international and non-international armed conflicts see J-M. Henckaerts and L. Doswald-Beck, *Customary International Humanitarian Law: Volume I: Rules* (ICRC: Cambridge University Press, 2005).

69 *Prosecutor v Tadic*, Judgment, IT-94-1-A, 15 July 1999.

70 R. Cryer, 'The Fine Art of Friendship: The *Jus in Bello* in Afghanistan' (2002) 7 *JCSL* 37.

71 K.A. Johnston, 'Transformations of Conflict Status in Libya' (2012) 17 *JCSL* 81.

6.9   Belligerent occupation

The application of the law of armed conflict ceases upon the close of hostilities with the exception of the continued occupation of enemy territories, when it continues to apply even if military operations have ceased. Belligerent occupation is the 'occupation of enemy territory, that is, when a belligerent in an armed conflict is in control of some of the adversary's territory and is directly responsible for administering the territory'.[72]

Belligerent occupation has been around since the nineteenth century. Before that, when a state captured enemy territory it merely treated it as its own, by right of conquest. Increasing discomfort with this position led to the development of a regime of belligerent occupation. With a strengthening *jus ad bellum* belligerent occupation can be a very important aspect of the laws of war. Articles 2(3) and 2(4) of the UN Charter require the peaceful settlement of disputes and the non-use of force in international relations, which signifies that the acquisition of title to territory by force is impermissible. This can be seen, for example, in the Security Council's reaction to the attempt by Iraq to forcibly annex Kuwait; an attempt declared null and void by the Security Council.[73] The law of belligerent occupation continues to be applicable to the territories occupied by Israel in the Six Day War of 1967.[74] Most recently, the law of belligerent occupation has been applied in Iraq by the US/UK (2003–2004). However, it has done so subject to certain modifications brought in by operation of mandatory Security Council resolutions.

After the invasion of Iraq in March 2003 the law of belligerent occupation (primarily governed by the Hague Regulations 1907, and the Fourth Geneva Convention 1949) was applied by the US and the UK (by forming a Coalition Provisional Authority – CPA) at least until mid-2004 when power was handed over to the interim Iraqi government. The occupation was recognised by the Security Council in Resolution 1483 of 2003. It is clear that specific aspects of the law of

---

72 UK, *Manual of the Law of Armed Conflict, supra* note 5, 274. See generally Y. Dinstein, *The International Law of Belligerent Occupation* (Cambridge University Press, 2009).

73 UNSC Res 662 (1990).

74 On the application of the Fourth Geneva Convention to the occupied territories, see for example UNSC Res 237 (1967), UNSC Res 1397 (2002) and UNGA Res 58/97 (2003). See also *Legal Consequences of the Construction of a Wall in the Occupied Palestinian Territory, supra* note 58, para 90.

occupation were used by the CPA, for example as a legal basis upon which to detain thousands of Iraqis deemed to be security threats.[75] However, the problems in applying the law of occupation to a situation of regime change (the removal of Saddam Hussein and his Baathist government and its replacement by an elected government) and state building are manifest given the basic principles upon which the law of belligerent occupation rests.

The basic principle governing the law of belligerent occupation is that sovereignty does not pass to the occupant, so the occupying state cannot treat the territory as its own. The occupants administer the territory until withdrawal. This is reflected in the Hague Regulations of 1907:

> The authority of the legitimate power having passed into the hands of the occupant, the latter shall take all the measures in his power to restore, and ensure, as far as possible, public order and safety, while respecting, unless absolutely prevented, the laws in force in the country.[76]

This provision is difficult to apply in the case of long-term occupations such as Israel's occupation of the Palestinian territories. An Israeli court has stated that in long administrations an occupant must ensure growth, change and development, so an occupant is entitled to develop industry, commerce, agriculture, health and welfare.[77]

In the occupation of Iraq it is clear that the CPA went beyond mere administration of the territory to act as sovereign, for example, in the privatisation of public utilities.[78] Furthermore, the policy of lustration, namely the removal from power of members of the former regime – the 'de-Ba'athification' of Iraq – by the CPA in 2003 seems at odds with the law, although it follows the example of the de-Nazification of Germany after the Second World War.[79] It follows from Article 43 that, as far as possible, administrative life should go on as uninterrupted and, furthermore, there are provisions in the Fourth Geneva Convention preventing the alteration of the status of judges and public

---

75 Arts 41–43 GC IV 1949.

76 Art 43 Regulations Respecting the Laws and Customs of War on Land, annexed to Hague Convention IV Respecting the Laws and Customs of War on Land 1907.

77 *Co-operative Society Case* (1984) 14 *Israel Year Book of Human Rights* 30.

78 C. McCarthy, 'The Paradox of the International Law of Military Occupation' (2005) 10 *JCSL* 43 at 51–5.

79 *Ibid.*, 54.

officials, although public officials can be removed from their posts if they do not wish to work for the occupant.[80]

In order to overcome the limitations of the laws of belligerent occupation, which, it should be borne in mind, did not prevent, nor were seen as a reason to prevent the reconstruction of Japan and Germany after the Second World War, the occupiers of Iraq secured the adoption of Security Council Resolution 1483. This Resolution not only endorsed the military presence and occupation of Iraq by the US and the UK, it also appeared to empower the CPA, under Chapter VII of the UN Charter, 'to advance efforts to restore and establish national and local institutions for representative governance, including working together to facilitate a process leading to an internationally recognized, representative government of Iraq'; to facilitate the 'reconstruction of key infrastructure, in cooperation with other international organizations'; to promote 'economic reconstruction and the conditions for sustainable development, including through coordination with national and regional organizations, as appropriate, civil society, donors and the international financial institutions . . .'; and to encourage 'international efforts to promote legal and judicial reform'.[81]

6.10   Role of the ICRC

The ICRC is a direct successor to the organisation set up as a result of Henry Dunant's initiative in the mid-nineteenth century. It is a private Swiss organisation having an international function; its Swiss identity helping to ensure the ICRC's neutrality, which 'plays a vital role in securing the trust of the parties to armed conflicts in the performance of its humanitarian functions'.[82]

These functions include 'supervision, neutral intermediation and provision of relief'.[83] The 'supervisory work of the ICRC during armed conflicts involves visiting prisoners of war, civilian internees and occupied territories in order to monitor and encourage the proper implementation of international humanitarian norms'.[84] If the ICRC

---

80 Art 54 GC IV 1949.

81 UNSC Res 1483 (2003), para 8.

82 McCoubrey, *supra* note 1, 43.

83 *Ibid.*, 44; citing Article VI of the Statutes of the International Red Cross.

84 McCoubrey, *supra* note 1, 45. See Art 126 GC III 1949; Art 143 GC IV 1949.

discovers breaches of the Geneva Conventions it will draw them to the attention of the relevant party and urge them to comply – in extreme circumstances it might make public denunciations, which it did, for example, over the conditions in internment camps in Bosnia in the 1990s.[85]

Hilaire McCoubrey explains the reason for the ICRC's reticence to make its judgements public:

> The ICRC is properly concerned that its role as neutral intermediary, enabling it to gain access to the victims whose protection it seeks to advance and facilitate and to urge full compliance with humanitarian law, should be preserved, and not compromised or destroyed by the adoption of an adversarial posture. This approach over the years achieved many notable successes, as well as meeting with some inevitable failures.[86]

The ICRC's supervisory function involves providing a Central Tracing Agency to maintain records and supply information relating to individuals captured, detained, killed or injured in armed conflict. Its relief work includes the provision of Red Cross parcels to PoWs, but also the delivery of humanitarian supplies to civilians.[87] In addition, the ICRC has the general responsibility of improving and disseminating international humanitarian law.[88]

6.11   Conclusion

The first object of international law is to preserve peace and security, thereby necessitating the construction of collective security organisations and laws regulating when force can be used in international relations. However, armed conflicts still happen and so, pragmatically, international humanitarian law has been developed to reduce the savagery of this dark side of the human condition, and it has largely done so through a neutral approach – evidenced by the equality of application of the law to both parties irrespective of the causes of war, and in the neutral approach of the ICRC which contrasts with the judgemental and sometimes punitive character of the UN.

---

85 McCoubrey, *supra* note 1, 46.

86 *Ibid.*, 46–7.

87 *Ibid.*, 48.

88 *Ibid.*, 49.

Inevitably the law is ridden with contradictory principles – of military necessity and humanity; of distinction and proportionality; and of great devastation and protection of the environment. In many ways the law is a valiant attempt to reconcile these principles but, because of the compromises it reaches, the law is only able to castigate the obvious breaches – the intentional (as opposed to accidental) killing of women and children for instance; while those more insidious violations such as the targeting of TV stations, bridges, convoys and civilian areas where fighters might be located seem to escape clear censure. Proportionality is too indeterminate a principle to prevent considerable, and in terms of the law, justifiable collateral damage. An increase in compliance mechanisms, in addition to the role played in this regard by the international criminal tribunals, would help. Michael Meyer has written that states are considering the 'possible functions of [a] . . . compliance system in more depth, including, for example, periodic reporting, fact-finding, early warnings, urgent appeals, non-binding legal opinions and, importantly, a possible format for a regular dialogue on . . . compliance among states'.[89]

Nevertheless, despite inherent problems, the law does set standards against which the most horrific acts can be judged and the perpetrators punished. However, the greatest problem besetting the law of armed conflict is the fact that reciprocity is largely absent from modern conflict. This is most obviously the case in an existential conflict between a government and rebels, where the victor is intent on eliminating the vanquished. The same animosity prevails in transnational conflicts between states and terrorist organisations. The last bastion of reciprocity – between states engaged in international armed conflict – is also under threat given the vast differences in military technology between developed states and developing states, where the former can strike at the latter without too much danger, leaving the latter to resort to unlawful means either against the attacking state (for example by mistreating the rare captured pilot) or against foreign nationals or, indeed, against its own citizens.

---

89 M. Meyer, 'The International Committee of the Red Cross and the Initiative to Strengthen Legal Protection for Victims of Armed Conflicts', in Harvey, Summers and White (eds), *supra* note 25.

7 Post-conflict law

7.1 Introduction

This chapter is concerned with identifying the legal framework applicable to the post-conflict stage (sometimes known as the *jus post bellum*) where parties and international actors are primarily concerned with establishing peace and security (normally within a state) and in the longer-term with rebuilding a state that is peaceful internally and externally.

The building blocks of peaceful international relations have been, and continue to be, states. States remain the primary form within which peoples organise themselves. Inter-state peace – the condition of peaceful relations between states – is premised on the existence of stable states. Over the centuries in the search for peace, governments have realised that a system of stable states necessitates a condition of peace within states – intra-state peace. International thinking and, somewhat more reluctantly, international law, have moved from the position of maintaining stability between states, to considering the form and function of states in order to ensure peace within states.[1]

Following the writings of Immanuel Kant formulated at the end of the eighteenth century, democratic peace theory argues that, since democracies do not wage war on each other, a world consisting solely of democratic states would be a peaceful one.[2] The problem with this position is that democracy, like beauty, is in the eye of the beholder. Nevertheless, international law is slowly shifting from the position that effective government provides the key to stable states, towards the idea of the state being based on self-determination, the true expression of

---

1 See generally N. Tsagourias and N.D. White, *Collective Security: Theory, Law and Practice* (Cambridge University Press, 2013) chapter 9.

2 I. Kant, *Perpetual Peace and Other Essays on History and Morals* (Indianapolis: Hackett, 1983) 113.

the people, reflected in accountable and representative government founded on respect for human rights.

7.2   Jus post bellum?

A central issue is whether the greater attention given to post-conflict states has led or, more realistically given that the subject is at an early stage of development, should lead to the creation of a third limb of international law to complement the *jus ad bellum* (more broadly the law of peace) and the *jus in bello* (more broadly the law of war). The arguments for a *jus post bellum* have been more fully rehearsed elsewhere,[3] and will not be recounted in full here given the approach of the present author, stated elsewhere, that we are 'dealing, not necessarily with a new area of law (there are after all plenty of human rights and humanitarian norms), but with an emerging legal regime'.[4]

In a sense the argument for a *jus post bellum* is a historical one and there is some evidence that, when the just war doctrine prevailed in medieval times, there was also a just peace doctrine that required the return of wrongfully acquired territory plus the payment of compensation to the just victor.[5] This so-called *jus victoriae* is an early version of the *jus post bellum*, but one which was lost in the eighteenth and nineteenth centuries when war was followed by peace treaties under which the victor claimed the spoils, and as many spoils as it could extract, out of the defeated state, including territories and colonies. In this period the position was that once a peace treaty was signed the former warring states returned to the law of peace; thus the only division necessary was a binary one where either the law of peace or the law of war applied.

In the modern era the *jus in bello* (in its more modern guise of international humanitarian law or the law of armed conflict) is no longer entirely separate from the rest of international law, rather it is *lex specialis*, in other words a set of additional and specific rules that regulate the conduct of hostilities when an armed conflict breaks out.

---

3 See generally C. Stahn and J. Kleffner (eds), *Jus Post Bellum: Towards a Law of Transition From Conflict to Peace* (The Hague: Asser Press, 2008).

4 N.D. White and D. Klaasen, 'An Emerging Legal Regime?' in N.D. White and D. Klaasen (eds), *The UN, Human Rights and Post Conflict Situations* (Manchester University Press, 2005) 1 at 2.

5 S. Neff, 'Conflict Termination and Peace-Making in the Law of Nations: A Historical Perspective' in C. Stahn and J. Kleffner, *supra* note 3, 77.

The continued relevance of the law of armed conflict is due to the purposes it serves – to mitigate the effects of warfare (including the protection of civilians). It is in this way that it could be argued that there is a need for a *jus post bellum* – not as an outdated attempt to add a 'third' limb of law, but as a response to the specific needs of the post-conflict state, which include its vulnerability and lack of capacity (for instance, in policing, prison facilities or in basic nutrition and education).

However, the position taken here is that there is a new legal *regime* developing in relation to post-conflict situations but this does not mean a new set of stand-alone laws rather a fusion and development of existing norms drawn from many areas of international law. According to Stephen Krasner, regimes are 'sets of implicit or explicit principles, norms, rules, and decision-making procedures around which actors' expectations converge in a given area of international relations'.[6] In the area of post-conflict situations those converging laws range from general principles of law such as sovereignty, self-determination, non-intervention and the non-use of force to specific rules of international humanitarian law, international human rights law, international criminal law, refugee law, development law and even financial law.

The newness of the law is found in how these many norms can be made to work in the complex and changing post-conflict environment. As abstract laws are applied and conflicts of norms emerge, then there may arise the need for new rules or new rules about rules, as post-conflict law develops from a rudimentary system of primary rules. By this method we avoid the simple urge to hold up the list of human rights found, for instance, in the Universal Declaration of Human Rights 1948, and declare that these are all immediately applicable in a post-conflict state where violence is still endemic and the state has largely been destroyed; for, as bluntly stated by Martti Koskenniemi, this 'provides no more guidance than does a general commitment to the good'.[7]

---

6 S. Krasner, 'Structural Causes and Regime Consequences: Regimes as International Variables' (1982) 36 *International Organization* 184 at 186.

7 M. Koskenniemi, 'Whose Tolerance? Which Democracy?' in G.H. Fox and B.R. Roth (eds), *Democratic Governance and International Law* (Cambridge University Press, 2000) 437.

7.3   Peace agreements and international law

Peace agreements, representing the focal point of efforts to bring a settlement about by peaceful means in accordance with Article 1(1) of the UN Charter, should be the basis of bringing into the post-conflict state applicable international laws. Although inter-state peace agreements are still negotiated in the modern era, the vast majority of peace agreements concern the establishment of peace within a war-torn state. Practice tends to indicate that these intra-state peace agreements are increasingly being shaped by international law.[8]

As Christine Bell points out, intra-state peace agreements are often structured as legal documents using legal language that appears to bind the parties; but she admits that such agreements defy traditional classification, sitting somewhere between an international treaty and the basis for a national constitution.[9] This is due to the fact that the conflicts they bring to an end have both internal and international elements, meaning that they perform the role of a treaty between states and a constitution for the peaceful state that is expected to emerge from the internecine disorder. Of course, if the peace agreement is purely inter-state then the traditional law of treaties applies, but most modern peace agreements involve at their core an agreement between the internal factions, which is often guaranteed by outside states (who may also have been involved in the conflict) and brokered or otherwise supported by international organisations.

While states are bound by treaties to which they are parties,[10] the question remains whether warring factions within a state can be viewed as subjects of international law, capable of bearing duties under international law. Belligerents and insurgents meeting quite strict criteria (for example the control of territory) have been viewed as subjects of international law (for example the Confederate side in the American Civil War),[11] and have been subject to *jus in bello* obligations; and those peoples fighting for self-determination (for example the Palestinian people) are recognised as subjects of international law for certain purposes,[12] but what of insurgents that fall short of these

---

8 C. Bell, 'Peace Agreements: Their Nature and Legal Status', (2006) 100 *AJIL* 373 at 373–5.

9 *Ibid.*, 378.

10 Arts 2–3, 26 Vienna Convention on the Law of Treaties 1969.

11 I. Brownlie, *Principles of Public International Law* (7th edn, Oxford University Press, 2008) 63.

12 *Ibid.*, 62–3.

categories, such as the Bosnian Serbs during the Bosnian Conflict or UNITA during the Angolan Civil War? The argument can become tautological – that such armed groups are subjects of international law because they (are allowed to) sign peace agreements. However, this does not explain why they are subjects and what other rights and duties they have.[13]

Debates about the binding force of provisions in peace agreements miss the point about the way in which international law works to shape expectations and behaviour using normative instruments containing 'soft' and 'hard' obligations. Bell questions whether the 'binding' or 'non-binding' nature of the peace agreement affects compliance. Other factors, such as the legitimacy of the agreement in terms of its inclusiveness of indigenous groups, and the processes of debate and diplomacy that led to it, as well as the support of the regional and international community towards it, are more important in making an agreement work.[14]

According to Bell peace agreements have different functions. The first function is that of an international treaty. This stabilises the inter-state peace as well as sets the framework for the internal processes within war-shattered states. For example, both the UN-brokered Cambodian Paris Peace Accords of 1991, and the US-brokered Dayton Peace Agreement of 1995, were primarily between states. State parties are in effect guaranteeing they will deliver their 'kindred' non-state actors.[15] Sometimes while states provide guarantees in the main treaty, annexes with specific agreements will apply to the factions (as with Dayton), which are often very detailed on cease-fire, withdrawal, demobilisation, disarmament, demining, cantonment, and the role of any peacekeeping or stabilisation force.

The second function is that of a constitution. If the agreement plays a significant domestic legal role then it can more centrally include non-state actors as part of the social contract element of the agreement. For example, the largely indigenous South African peace process, starting with the National Peace Accord of 1991, led to the interim constitution of post-apartheid country, containing details not only on individual rights, and the institutions of a state, but also on the assimilation of

---

13 Bell, *supra* note 8, 384.
14 *Ibid.*
15 *Ibid.*, 389–90.

former factions. Most often such agreements are not permanent con-
stitutions and are, therefore, subject to change once a new (elected)
government is in place, which leads to debates about the values governing the state. Respect for the international legal principles of self-
determination and non-intervention should mean that such debates
and decisions are internal ones for the representatives of the people,
but the dangers of external actors imposing 'alien' values are all too
evident from the failures of the Dayton Accords to deliver a truly independent and representative federal Bosnian state.[16]

7.4   Outside involvement in post-conflict states

The exercise of the right to self-determination by colonised peoples
led to the creation of many new states in the 1960s,[17] representing a
major change in international relations in the post-Cold War period.
However, most of these decolonised states were weak, especially in
Africa, necessitating the first fraught UN intra-state intervention, in
the Congo in 1960–1964. These new states could not upset the balance of power between East and West, although the development of
the Non-Aligned Movement of developing states did provide a forum
for formulating their (largely unsuccessful) demands for a more equi-
table world, evidenced for instance in calls for a New International
Economic Order in the 1970s.[18]

Furthermore, these new states were extremely jealous of their new-
found sovereignty and argued for a strong norm of non-intervention.[19]
While understandably rejecting any return to colonialism, these new
states were unable to prevent new forms of domination and intervention, whether economic (especially by multinational corporations), or
military (particularly evident in superpower zones of influence, but
also in contested countries such as Vietnam and Angola). Developing
countries, especially in Africa, continue to have porous and often
disputed frontiers, and often ineffective and corrupt governments,
thus reflecting a formal type of sovereignty, as distinct from the

---

16 See generally D. Chandler, *Bosnia: Faking Democracy After Dayton* (2nd edn, London: Pluto,
    2000).
17 As recognised in UNGA Res 1514 (1960).
18 GA Res 3201 (1974).
19 GA Res 2131 (1965).

more powerful form of Westphalian sovereignty found in developed states.[20]

The failure of some of these states (for example the Congo in the 1960s and again in the 1990s, and Somalia in the 1990s), and the abuses committed against their own people by others (for example Uganda and Kampuchea in the 1970s), have led to so-called humanitarian interventions by states (by Tanzania in Uganda and Vietnam in Kampuchea) and, more legitimately, by international organisations (for example by the UN in Somalia).[21] Indeed, given the rejection of colonialism and imperialism as legitimate forms of outside intervention, the only legitimate form of outside involvement (as least one that involves post-conflict peace-building) must be undertaken by established international organisations, either universal such as the UN or regional such as the African Union (AU), OAS, European Union (EU), Arab League and the Association of South Eastern Nations (ASEAN).[22]

Peacekeeping during the Cold War was initially designed to secure and supervise an established cease-fire between states, as with the first peacekeeping force (the United Nations Emergency Force (UNEF)) created by the General Assembly in 1956 to supervise the cease-fire and withdrawal of foreign forces from Suez.[23] This was extended in 1960 to keeping (or rather enforcing) the peace within a collapsing post-colonial state in the case of the United Nations Operation in the Congo (ONUC),[24] although the force placed within Cyprus in 1964 reverted to the traditional type of consensual, non-interventionist force for which the UN has become well-known.[25] This orthodox concept of peacekeeping was firmly grounded on the principles of consent, impartiality (often interpreted to signify neutrality), and limited use of force (seen as defence of peacekeepers and their equipment).[26]

---

20 A. Anghie, *Imperialism, Sovereignty and the Making of International Law* (Cambridge University Press, 2004) 236–44.

21 On the legality of humanitarian interventions see C. Gray, 'The Use of Force for Humanitarian Purposes' in N.D. White and C. Henderson (eds), *Research Handbook on International Conflict and Security Law* (Cheltenham: Edward Elgar Publishing, 2013) 229.

22 See generally R. Caplan, *International Governance of War-Torn Territories* (Oxford University Press, 2005).

23 UNGA Res 999-1001 (1956).

24 UNSC Res 143 (1960), UNSC Res 146 (1960), UNGA Res 1474 (1960), UNSC Res 169 (1961).

25 UNSC Res 186 (1964), UNSC Res 353 (1974).

26 See N.D. White, 'Peacekeeping or War Fighting?' in White and Henderson, *supra* note 21, 572.

Intervention by the UN changed in the late 1980s and early 1990s, with operations becoming multifunctional by combining peacekeeping with limited peace-building, usually centred upon the holding of elections as the pivotal event between conflict and a stable state. Such operations were a mixed success, with a number failing because the electoral process did not engage the factions sufficiently to prevent a fresh outbreak of fighting. Since the Brahimi Report of 2000 we have seen the emergence of more integrated and more extensive UN peace operations, which combine peacekeeping with more ambitious peace-building, consisting of much more than the basic introduction of Western-style democracy to an often alien environment.

The post-Cold War peace operations, where peacekeeping was combined with peace-making under the principles of consent, impartiality and the limited use of force, started with the UN operation in Namibia in 1989. In the early 1990s the UN rapidly developed a multi-dimensional peacekeeping and peace-building model, a number of examples of which were successful in achieving their more ambitious mandates, for example in Nicaragua, El Salvador, Cambodia, and Mozambique, although a number struggled, most notably the force in Angola.

The Brahimi Report of 2000 developed and defined the three principal elements of UN peace operations to include peace-making; peacekeeping as traditionally defined, and thirdly, peace-building, namely those 'activities undertaken on the far side of conflict to reassemble the foundations of peace and provide the tools for building on those foundations something that is more than just the absence of war'. It includes the reintegration of former combatants into civilian life; strengthening the rule of law (for example, police, judiciary and prisons); improving respect for human rights; providing technical assistance for democratic development; and promoting conflict resolution and reconciliation techniques.[27]

Undoubtedly with failures such as the mission in Angola in mind, the Brahimi Report recognised that free and fair elections are just part of a process of building 'governance institutions', democratisation, the protection of human rights and the development of civil

---

27 Report of the Panel on United Nations Peace Operations (Brahimi Report), UN Doc A/55/305-S/2000/809, paras 10–13.

society.[28] The peace operation aims to develop a partnership with the local population and time is taken in developing political and civil processes. The Report recognised that in a number of early peace operations 'hasty elections' took the 'place of finding legitimate interlocutors'.[29]

The principles of international law outlined in this chapter require that once it is clear that the people have exercised, and are able to continue to exercise, their right to self-determination (which does not mean simply holding elections), and that secure institutions and processes are in place, then the sovereignty and independence of the people and the country should be respected and the operation withdrawn, unless a small residual operation is left in a more symbolic role. An essential element is that the process engages the local population and ensures that they are the main stakeholders as well as the beneficiaries of the process.[30] Fundamentally, the process should allow for the local population to shape the society, not for it to be shaped by outside actors.

However, Roland Paris has argued that 'most international organisa-tions engaged in peacebuilding have internalised the broadly liberal political and economic values of the wealthy and powerful indus-trialised democracies', and have in effect 'transplanted' those values (elections, civil and political rights and market reforms) into weak countries in which peace operations have been located. This is most evident in cases of 'proxy government' by the UN in Kosovo and East Timor first established in 1999, though it is not only in these obvious cases, but also arguably in other multifunctional operations such as occurred in Cambodia and Mozambique. Paris argued that this process amounts to the 'globalisation of the very idea of what a state should look like and how it should act'.[31] It remains to be seen whether the UN Peacebuilding Commission, created in 2005 to develop integrated strategies for post-conflict rebuilding and recovery,

---

28 *Ibid.*, para 38.

29 Challenges Project, *Meeting the Challenges of Peace Operations: Cooperation and Coordination* (Stockholm: Elanders Gotab, 2005) 48.

30 B. Pouligny, 'Local Ownership' in V. Chetail (ed.), *Post-Conflict Peacebuilding: A Lexicon* (Oxford University Press, 2009) 174.

31 R. Paris, 'International Peacekeeping and the "Mission Civilisatrice"' (2002) 28 *Review of International Studies* 637, 638–9.

will usher in a renewed impartiality, as well as effectiveness, to peace operations.[32]

7.5   Peace-building and self-determination

While Roland Paris may have a point in a number of instances of post-conflict rebuilding under UN and other auspices (particularly in the 1990s), the question remains whether this is based on a complete, or merely selective application, of relevant international law. Pivotal in this regard is the right of self-determination, first embodied as a legal principle in the decolonisation period of the 1960s and embodied in General Assembly resolutions, which endowed colonised peoples with the right to both political and economic independence (including permanent sovereignty over natural resources).[33] There will continue to be the occasional case of new states being created through external self-determination; for example by consent as in the case of the independence of Southern Sudan in 2011 in accordance with the Comprehensive Peace Agreement for the Sudan of 2005. However, external self-determination will normally be achieved by protecting the independence of an existing state in a peace agreement.

The importance of self-determination as a fundamental principle of the *jus post bellum* becomes clear, but it must be considered alongside other fundamental principles of international law such as non-intervention. While international actors such as the UN will be concerned to rebuild the state, it can only establish the basic framework within which this should happen, a framework that enables the people to decide on the form of government and other political structures and processes, its economic and social structures. That framework within which the UN and the post-conflict state should work is shaped by basic principles of international law – respect for political and economic independence, territorial integrity, but also respect for fundamental human rights.

In the post-Cold War era it is the internal aspect of self-determination that is mainly addressed by peace agreements. This is the case with the other peace process in Sudan located in the (unfulfilled) Darfur Peace Agreement of 2006, which envisaged greater autonomy for the people of Darfur within Sudan. This aspect of self-determination is

---

32 See World Summit Outcome Document UNGA Res 60/1 (2005), para 102.
33 UNGA Res 1514 (1960), UNGA Res 1803 (1962), UNGA Res 2627 (1970).

buttressed by minority rights,[34] the rights of indigenous peoples,[35] and so-called 'democratic' rights (of which there are several – freedoms of expression, thought, opinion, association, assembly),[36] but these, by themselves, do not fully embody the idea of self-determination in the new era, despite the claims of some jurists.[37] Such a focus on civil and political rights fails to take account of the economic aspects of self-determination, which are specifically protected by core economic and social rights. Furthermore, the key to peace agreements and the peace process is the establishment of power-sharing representative political institutions (underpinned by freedoms of expression, opinion, association and assembly), which will enable decisions to be made about the economic and social future of the state.

Early post-Cold War peace agreements tended to reflect a vision of self-determination as being best delivered by means of elections. For example the Cambodian Peace Agreements of 1991 declared that the:

> Cambodian people shall have the right to determine their own political future through the free and fair election of a constituent assembly, which will draft and approve a new Cambodian Constitution in accordance with Article 23 and transform itself into a legislative assembly, which will create the new Cambodian Government. This election will be held under United Nations auspices in a neutral political environment with full respect for the national sovereignty of Cambodia.[38]

There is no guarantee that this by itself will produce a representative government accountable to the people in case of human rights abuse or neglect (as borne out by subsequent events in Cambodia). This has led to greater levels of international intervention in later peace processes, but with this there are concomitant problems of interference with genuine processes of self-determination.

Encouraging signs of the UN moving towards a more even-handed approach are reflected in its increased emphasis on promotion of the 'rule of law' within post-conflict countries alongside 'democracy'.

---

34 Art 27 International Covenant on Civil and Political Rights 1966.
35 UNGA 61/295 (2007).
36 Arts 18, 19, 21, 22, 25 International Covenant on Civil and Political Rights 1966.
37 T.M. Franck, 'The Emerging Right to Democratic Governance', (1992) 86 *AJIL* 46.
38 Art 12 Final Act of the Paris Conference on Cambodia 1991.

Indeed, while the latter dominated discourse of the 1990s,[39] the rule of law has come to the fore in the twenty-first century.[40] Furthermore, in the World Summit Outcome Document of 2005 the rule of law was recognised, alongside human rights and democracy, as belonging to 'universal and indivisible core values and principles of the United Nations'.[41] According to the UN Secretary General the rule of law is a 'principle of governance in which all persons, institutions and entities, public and private, including the state itself, are accountable to laws that are publicly promulgated, equally enforced and independently adjudicated, and which are consistent with international human rights law and standards'.[42]

7.6   International human rights law and post-conflict rebuilding

There has been considerable argument concerning the legal principles and norms applicable to the post-conflict rebuilding phase, the content of the *jus post bellum*.[43] There are numerous international legal regimes that are, in principle, applicable to the post-conflict stage, and though they are not necessarily in conflict with each other, debates about their applicability can lose sight of the importance of general principles of international law such as self-determination and non-intervention, but also fundamental values such as peace and security.

It must not be forgotten that the primary purpose of international conflict and security law, restoring peace and security, still persists in the post-conflict phase, although the blind pursuit of peace without reference to justice is neither appropriate in legal terms nor effective.

---

39 On the latter see UNSG, 'Agenda for Democratization' (UN, 1996). For critical evaluation of the application of democracy to Afghanistan see W. Malley, 'Democracy and Legitimation: Challenges in the Reconstruction of Political Processes in Afghanistan' in B. Bowden, H. Charlesworth, and J. Farrall (eds), *The Role of International Law in Rebuilding Societies* (Cambridge University Press, 2009) 111.

40 J. Farrall, 'Impossible Expectations? The UN Security Council's Promotion of the Rule of Law After Conflict' in Bowden, Charlesworth and Farrall (eds), *supra* note 39, 134. See generally W. Mason (ed.), *The Rule of Law in Afghanistan: Missing in Inaction* (Cambridge University Press, 2011).

41 UNGA Res 60/1 (2005) para 119.

42 UNSG, 'The Rule of Law and Transitional Justice in Conflict and Post-Conflict Societies', UN Doc S/2004/616 (2004) para 6. See generally L. Grenfell, *Promoting the Rule of Law in Post-Conflict States* (Cambridge University Press, 2013).

43 See C. Stahn, 'Jus Post Bellum: Mapping the Discipline' in Stahn and Kleffner, *supra* note 3, 93.

Alongside concerns for peace and security, principles of human rights law (and where applicable, international humanitarian law), international criminal law and transitional justice play an important role in post-conflict rebuilding.

International humanitarian law is applicable during armed conflict, and thus is primarily applicable to the *jus in bello* phase rather than the *jus post bellum*. However, if violence persists, or flares up again in the post-conflict phase and reaches the level of an internal armed conflict, then international humanitarian law (the *jus in bello*) applies to the parties to a conflict, and also to a UN peacekeepers' operation if they engage as combatants.[44]

Thus, humanitarian law does not play a significant role in a *jus post bellum*.[45] In identifying a body of applicable law, regard must be had to the priority of ensuring that peace and security in a fragile state is established, maintained and then improved. Improvement will only occur if justice is incorporated, not only by forms of transitional justice to address past atrocities, but also by recognising the basic human rights of the population, and the obligations not only of the host state, but those outside states and organisations involved in the rebuilding process.[46]

The primary obligation to respect and protect human rights is placed on the post-conflict state itself. Unless the state is already a party to international human rights treaties, its obligations at this stage are derived from customary international law covering those basic rights drawn from across the human rights spectrum – the right to life, freedom from torture or other forms of cruel, inhuman or degrading treatment; freedom from slavery or other similar practices; freedom from discrimination based on ethnic, religious, racial grounds or on the basis of sex; freedom from arbitrary arrest or detention; and basic due process rights (covering arrest, detention, and trial);[47] as well as the rights to food, water, shelter, medicine (health), and basic education.[48] Given that internal violence in the past may have been caused

---

44 UNSG's Bulletin, 'Observance by United Nations Forces of International Humanitarian Law', UN Doc ST/SGB/1999/13.

45 There is also the occasional application of the law of occupation to intervening states (but not to organisations) – see Chapter 6.

46 R. Caplan, 'Transitional Administration' in Chetail, *supra* note 30, 359 at 363.

47 Brownlie, *supra* note 11, 562–4.

48 See Committee on Economic, Social and Cultural Rights, 'General Comment 3: The Nature of States Parties Obligations – Article 2(1) of the Covenant', UN Doc E/1991/23, para 10.

by the denial of group or minority rights then, as well as enforcing the principle of non-discrimination, the protection of cultural, minority, and other group rights is essential in the post-conflict state.[49]

Once these basic rights are secured, the post-conflict state can look to become a party to the main human rights treaties, including the two international covenants on human rights, in order to realise the full range of human rights. If already a party to such treaties, the state party may consider derogating from some of the derogable rights,[50] but only if the life of the nation remains threatened by violence extending beyond the peace treaty. Recognising that a state can move over time from a basic regime of human rights protection towards a full regime allows that state, and the international community, to place initial emphasis on security without denying the basic principles of justice.

In addition to having obligations not to breach the basic human rights of its citizens and other individuals within its jurisdiction, the post-conflict state has positive obligations to take steps to protect the human rights of those individuals from breach by third parties such as armed groups that are neither state agents nor under the effective control of the state. This very important principle was established by the Inter-American Court of Human Rights in relation to a number of Latin American 'dirty wars' in which individuals were 'disappeared' by 'death squads'.[51]

These 'due diligence' obligations extend to third states and international organisations, whose agents are present in the post-conflict state in order to help its reconstruction. These states and organisations must ensure that they act with due diligence to prevent as far as possible the violation of human rights, by, for example, protecting civilians within their control (for instance, in UN bases or camps, detention centres, and arguably, in their areas of deployment) from attack by private actors, or from other potential sources of physical harm such as uncleared ordnance. Furthermore, the UN Security Council has committed peacekeepers to protect civilians under existential threat in their areas of deployment.[52] The duty on peacekeepers to protect

---

49 Art 27, International Covenant on Civil and Political Rights 1966; Art 15, International Covenant on Economic, Social and Cultural Rights 1966.
50 Art 4(1), International Covenant on Civil and Political Rights 1966.
51 *Velasquez Rodriguez case,* 1988 Ser. C, No. 4 (1988), para 172.
52 Starting with UNSC Res 1265 (1999).

in these circumstances is derived from UN Security Council decisions irrespective of any applicable human rights obligations.[53]

It follows that the UN and states sending troops have duties of prevention as well as duties not to commit violations of human rights. Although peacekeepers are acting extra-territorially, the human rights obligations of their sending states attach to them in circumstances where they exercise control over areas or over individuals.[54] This principle was suggested by the Human Rights Committee in 2004 when it stated that parties to the International Covenant on Civil and Political Rights must ensure the human rights of persons 'within the power or effective control of the forces of a State Party acting outside its territory ... such as forces constituting a national contingent of a State Party assigned to an international peace-keeping or peace-enforcement operation'.[55]

When the UN is in effective control of the conduct of peacekeepers (and it normally accepts that it is in such control in UN-commanded and UN-controlled peacekeeping operations),[56] responsibility for human rights violations lies with the organisation; while normally in coalitions authorised by the Security Council under Chapter VII, responsibility lies with contributing states.[57] The somewhat stricter test proposed in the ILC's Articles on the Responsibility of International Organisations 2011, namely that the organisations must have been in effective control of the *conduct* of state organs (such as soldiers or police officers) for responsibility to fall on the organisation,[58] seems to have added a degree of uncertainty over what had been established practice. Even though there is meant to be UN command and control of peace operations, the fact that military discipline remains with the troop-contributing nation, and that the governments of those nations

---

53 Most modern peacekeeping mandates require peacekeepers to protect civilians within their care and, where possible, within their areas of deployment – see, for example, UNSC Res 1542 (2004) para 7I(f) re the force in Haiti.

54 See European Court of Human Rights, *Al-Skeini v United Kingdom*, Judgment (App. No. 55721/07), 7 July 2011.

55 Human Rights Committee, General Comment 31, 'Nature of the General Legal Obligation on States Parties to the Covenant', UN Doc CCPR/C/21/Rev 1/Add.13 (2004), para 10.

56 I. Scobbie, 'International Organizations and International Relations' in R.J. Dupuy (ed.), *A Handbook on International Organizations* (Leiden: Martinus Nijhoff, 1999) 891.

57 But see European Court of Human Rights, *Behrami and Saramati v France, Germany and Norway*, Judgment (App. Nos. 71412/01 and 78166/01), 2007.

58 Art 7, Articles on the Responsibility of International Organizations, UN Doc. A/66/10 (2011).

will veto any controversial order, signifies that establishing that the UN is in effective control of specific conduct will be difficult.

Despite this potentially retrograde development, the ILC's Articles on the Responsibility of International Organisations clearly show that it is possible to attribute wrongful acts to the UN as well as troop-contributing countries, and such responsibility is based on the UN having duties under customary international law including ones to uphold and protect human rights. As an autonomous entity, having international legal personality, the UN is recognised as having rights and duties under international law.[59] Thus, human rights obligations in the context of peace operations have two potential sources: the treaty and customary obligations of sending states and the customary obligations of the UN.

The promotion and protection of civil and political rights, and economic, social, and cultural rights, is essential in developing fair and effective governance. Peace operations have to be careful not to protect and promote civil and political rights as a priority (whether for ideological or practical reasons). Only by so doing can the right to self-determination in both its political and economic aspects be protected. Of importance for the economic aspect of the right to self-determination are the tasks undertaken, in part, by peace operations of development and relief, which will include at the lowest level the meeting of basic needs (the fulfilment of the basic human rights to life, food, water, and shelter), and then the development of economic and social infrastructure. Clearly there is a danger of interfering in the choices a society might make about economic, social, and political development.

7.7   Transitional justice

A peaceful state can only be achieved by combining security with justice, though a certain priority can be given to peace and security in the transitional phase by, for instance, derogating from certain human rights if the situation remains one of genuine emergency. Nonetheless, short-term security can only delay the pursuit of justice for past atrocities, a notion recognised in the Rome Statute of the International Criminal Court, which allows the UN Security Council to temporarily

---

59 *Reparation for Injuries Suffered in the Service of the United Nations,* (1949) ICJ Rep 174 at 178; *Interpretation of the Agreement of 25 March 1951 between the WHO and Egypt,* (1980) ICJ Rep 73 at 89–90.

defer any investigation or prosecution of a case in the interests of peace and security.[60]

Indeed, there is increasing recognition that international criminal justice plays a very important role in post-conflict rebuilding. This is not only evidenced by the Rome Statute, which, in the preamble, clearly links serious criminal behaviour (the commission of war crimes, crimes against humanity, genocide and acts of aggression) with threats to peace and security. Furthermore, the Rome Statute recognises in Article 13 that the Security Council has significant powers of referral.[61] The Security Council's contribution to international criminal justice has been considerable, by the creation of international criminal tribunals (for Yugoslavia, Rwanda and Lebanon), and by the endorsement of hybrid tribunals,[62] which mix national and international elements. All of these institutions were created during or after periods of conflict within states, but they do not preclude national forms of criminal justice, involving criminal courts and truth commissions.

The difficulty in achieving a precise balance between establishing peace and pursuing justice is reflected in the debate about amnesties, which might be agreed between the former warring parties in exchange for coming to the negotiating table and agreeing peace. Although the UN has refused to endorse amnesties in Sierra Leone in 1999 and Angola in 2002, any claim that amnesties are now out of place in peace-building is over-stated.[63] As La Rosa and Philippe make clear:

> The ideal combination of criminal action and truth-seeking mechanism is often a mirage. Frequently, nothing changes. Inertia is one of the big challenges facing justice in post-conflict situations. Without going as far as blanket amnesties, very often there is no justice because there is no prosecution.[64]

While tempting to let sleeping dogs lie, the evidence suggests that a failure to address past atrocities will simply delay the need to find the truth, to determine accountability and to provide reparations to

---

60 Art 16, Rome Statute of the International Criminal Court 1998.

61 See the referrals in UNSC Res 1593 (2005) re the situation in Darfur; UNSC Res 1970 (2011) re the situation in Libya.

62 Hybrid tribunals in Bosnia, Cambodia, Kosovo, East Timor, Sierra Leone.

63 M. Freeman, *Necessary Evils: Amnesties and the Search for Justice* (Cambridge University Press, 2009) 88–109.

64 A-M. La Rosa and X. Philippe, 'Transitional Justice' in Chetail, *supra* note 30, 368 at 376.

victims. If not achieved in the immediate post-conflict stage, tackling injustice will have to occur at a later stage, when it will be more difficult to find the truth, to punish (or forgive) wrongdoers, and when it is too late to compensate victims. Simmering discontent and the entrenchment of victimhood for groups and their descendants will mean that the cycle of violence is not broken, at some point the peace will breakdown because of the failure to address past injustices.[65]

7.8   Conclusion

The re-establishment of peace within a war-torn state by whatever means are necessary (by, for example, supporting a despotic but effective government, or by granting amnesties to those accused of egregious violations of human rights) is no longer acceptable, either as a matter of policy or as a matter of law. Effective, but accountable and representative, government should be the aim of the state-building efforts of the UN and other legitimate international actors. Such governments are a product of self-determination and are likely to ensure the continued exercise of that right, and are more likely to be less violent internally, and more likely to be peaceful in their external relations.

Post-conflict law is essentially an application and development of basic principles of international law, combined with the application of more specific regimes. It has only been possible to consider some of these legal regimes in this chapter but they can be listed here to include aspects of international criminal law (combining with national courts and non-judicial mechanisms to provide transitional justice), refugee law, development law, financial law (governing the involvement of the World Bank for instance), institutional law (governing peacekeeping and peace-building by the UN and other organisations) and human rights law. Although the latter has weaknesses, particularly its application to outside actors, it is human rights law (including the right to self-determination), which provides the central legal template within which post-conflict states should develop.

---

65 D. Shelton, *Remedies in International Human Rights Law* (2nd edn, Oxford University Press, 2005) 14–15.

8 Peace and justice

8.1 Introduction

This will be a brief concluding chapter. It would be an exercise in hubris to suggest that detailed definitive conclusions can be drawn from what is, after all, an introductory text. This chapter will go back to three of the key questions raised throughout the book:

1. Has international conflict and security law achieved the purposes set out in Chapter 1?

2. What progress has international conflict and security law made towards securing both peace and justice?

3. What will/should be the future direction of international conflict and security law?

Some tentative conclusions are drawn under each question but the aim of this final chapter is not to give definitive answers but to provoke and perhaps guide debate. What follows are some suggested conclusions but readers will inevitably have drawn their own. Moreover, rather than repeating those conclusions drawn under each chapter, this final chapter considers the central theme of combining peace and justice, since it has been contended throughout that this is the ultimate aim of international conflict and security law.

This chapter is premised on the presupposition that the historical and political circumstances surrounding treaties and other agreements in international relations signify that there are no neat answers, nor perfectly coherent and consistent inter-locking legal regimes. However, it remains the case that those legal regimes analysed throughout the course of this book – principally the law of arms control, the law governing the use of force (*jus ad bellum*), the law of armed conflict (*jus in bello*), and post-conflict law (*jus post bellum*) all have the objective of regulating to limit violence between states, and increasingly between states and non-state actors, and between non-state actors themselves. Furthermore, the longer-term project is not simply to limit existential violence but to build a sustainable peace based on justice.

8.2   Achievements of international conflict and security law

In large part, laws and legal regimes are created to address serious social problems, by designating acts or omissions of legal persons (states, individuals, corporations . . .) as criminal or otherwise delictual. In other words this aspect of the law is aimed at tackling wrongs, evils, or more generally behaviour that threatens human cohabitation, development or even existence. International conflict and security law is directed at all these issues often at a fundamental level, for example in arms control law, which struggles to regulate the proliferation of the most destructive weapons in existence. In the area of armed conflict, international humanitarian law seeks to curb the excesses of warfare and reduce the suffering of combatants and provide protection for civilians. In general the limitation of violence is a pre-requisite to human development and in this sense international conflict and security law can be seen as a pre-condition to other forms of legal empowerment as well as regulation.

The paradox of this area of legal regulation is that it is at the same time fundamental and flawed, so that any sober evaluation of the law would naturally conclude that it has helped curb existential violence but it has not prevented massive and appalling aggression, atrocities, and disproportionate uses of kinetic force, which breach many of the fundamental principles of the legal regimes identified in this book. We cannot live without these rules, but without more effective enforcement and compliance (to cover both state and non-state actors such as corporations and armed groups) we will have to endure repeated violations of them.

The law is both idealised in one area (for example in the *jus ad bellum*'s insistence on the illegality of the use of force unless undertaken in self-defence or if sanctioned by a legitimate security community) and pragmatic in another (for example in the *jus in bello*'s recognition of the reality of warfare and military necessity). In purely philosophical terms this could be seen as contradictory, but the law is not always (indeed often) a product of pure reason, but fundamental laws in particular are a reflection of a social consensus or compacts at any particular time. Thus, the UN Charter of 1945, the Geneva Conventions of 1949, the NPT of 1968 and other treaties, customs and important instances of soft law (for example the Universal Declaration of Human Rights of 1948) represent the shared understandings or social contracts between states at the time and have been developed and adapted to respond to changing social conditions thereafter.

Part of that change is to recognise that international conflict and security law should not only be concerned with preserving the existence of states, by tackling inter-state breaches of the peace and threats to national security, but should address existential threats to individuals and groups within states on the basis that inter-state peace and intra-state peace are intertwined. State security and human security are not fully separable, although entrenched despotic regimes such as North Korea have proved to be durable and represent a threat to inter-state security as well as the human security of their own populations. Furthermore, there is no guarantee that democratic states, although more accountable to their populations, will not engage in aggressive war externally as evidenced by the misjudged invasion of Iraq in 2003 by the US and the UK. Although there are exceptions, the confluence of state and human security is not just a practical recognition that stable, accountable and representative states are the key to international peace and security, but a more idealised recognition that peace and justice are inter-linked and that, although peace may be prioritised in the short-term, longer-term peace cannot be achieved without justice.

8.3   Combining peace and justice

There is strong evidence that substantial moves have been made since the adoption of the UN Charter towards combining peace and security with justice. Some of these developments are summarised below, others will be found in the body of the book. It must not be thought, however, that the progress is linear or inevitable. There have been many setbacks and regressions, not only in practice where genocides still happen, but also in the law, for example in the unclear state of the right of self-defence against non-state actors. After the events of 9/11 in 2001 it is difficult to define with precision the extent of the right of self-defence against terrorist attacks or threats. Furthermore, there are quite fundamental structural and systemic weaknesses in the normative and institutional frameworks that will need to be addressed by states agreeing on new social compacts. For example, the right of veto, the wider membership of the Security Council, and the inequality under the NPT, reflect outdated privileges and hierarchies; while the uncertainty in the applicability of human rights during armed conflict reflect the problems in reconciling overlapping legal regimes, as well as different conceptions of justice.

Peace and justice are being forged together in the newest limb of international conflict and security law – post-conflict law or the *jus post bellum* – where peace-building combines security with self-determination, and re-assimilation with transitional justice. Peacekeepers in post-conflict situations are not just mandated to secure a cease-fire, but to protect civilians under threat and, above all, to protect the peace process.

Peace and justice are both found in the *jus ad bellum*, where defensive force or force sanctioned by the Security Council are the recognised just wars in the post-1945 world order, and in the *jus in bello*, where principles of humanity balance military necessity. It can be argued that these legal regimes need to tilt more towards justice, for example, by increasing the weight given to humanity and to the protection of civilians under the law of armed conflict. Some progress in this regard has recently been made in the *jus ad bellum* to fill the current significant gap in the legal order whereby egregious violations of human rights (amounting to systematic war crimes, crimes against humanity or genocide) do not give rise to direct responsibilities on states and international institutions under the UN Charter. The Security Council may act if it determines that such situations constitute a threat to the peace, or states may act unilaterally to intervene under the problematic and abused doctrine of humanitarian intervention, but neither of these avenues will necessarily lead to intervention to prevent or stop such atrocities. It is within this context, at the interface between collective security and international criminal/human rights law, that the doctrine of R2P (the responsibility to protect) is taking root.

R2P's origins are in the 2001 report of the Canadian government-appointed International Commission on Intervention and State Sovereignty (ICISS). Two premises underpinned ICISS's approach. First of all there was a presumption that 'state sovereignty implies responsibility', and that the 'primary responsibility for the protection

of its people lies with the state itself'. The idea of sovereignty as responsibility does not accord with the traditional concept of sovereignty as
one of exclusive jurisdiction and rights, but within the context of the
era of human rights, it is entirely justifiable. The second presumption
was that 'where a population is suffering harm, as a result of internal
war, insurgency, repression or state failure, and the state in question is
unwilling or unable to halt or avert it, the principle of non-intervention
yields to the international responsibility to protect'. Such an assertion
is more problematic in that it begs the question as to what is meant by
intervention, given that the Commission listed the elements of R2P as
the responsibility to react (including 'in extreme cases military intervention'), as well the responsibility to prevent and the responsibility to
rebuild. The Commission stressed that 'prevention is the single most
important dimension of the responsibility to protect', and therefore
requires greater commitment and resources.[1]

A strong argument can be made that the UN ought to act to prevent
genocide, crimes against humanity and other egregious violations of
human rights, either because there is a duty on states and therefore
on other actors, possessing rights and duties, to act within their legal
competences to prevent such violations of international law,[2] or simply
because such actions inherently undermine peace and security as well as
being international crimes. However, the only clear legitimate security
community that is able to react by authorising military action in such
circumstances is the Security Council. The Security Council's *discretionary* power to deal with threats to the peace under Chapter VII is difficult to reconcile with a *responsibility* to protect civilian populations.[3]

Nonetheless, in 2011 the Security Council appeared to be taking action
to tackle crimes against humanity in the context of increasing violence
within Libya, particularly the imminent attack on the rebel stronghold
of Benghazi by government forces. A detailed analysis of the Security
Council's responses shows it focused on its primary responsibility for
peace and security but it did combine this with R2P considerations.
The key is Resolution 1973 (2011), which authorised NATO to take
military action to impose a no-fly zone and to protect civilians under

---

1 ICISS, 'Responsibility to Protect' (International Development Centre, Ottawa, December 2001) xi.
2 See Art I of the Genocide Convention 1948, which obliges state parties to 'prevent and punish' the
   crime of genocide.
3 See N. Tsagourias and N.D. White, *Collective Security: Theory, Law and Practice* (Cambridge
   University Press, 2013) chapters 5 and 8.

imminent threat. In the circumstances of an existential threat to the civilian population of Benghazi the members of the Security Council were able to agree on Resolution 1973 on Libya, but only just, with ten votes in favour and five abstentions (Brazil, China, Germany, India and Russia). Those abstaining were not only the usual advocates of non-intervention (China and Russia) but other important states, each with a strong case for permanent membership themselves.[4]

The political change within the Security Council from the situation in Kosovo in 1999, when it could not agree on military action to protect the Kosovars,[5] to Libya in 2011 was marginal but sufficient to give the initial NATO action in Libya a sound legal basis. That marginal push may have been helped by the emergence in the early twenty-first century of the idea that there is a R2P on the part of the international community, when a state has failed to protect its population from crimes against humanity or other similar egregious acts.

In reviewing progress on R2P and its application to Libya, the UN Secretary General Ban Ki-moon attempted to reconcile the discretionary powers of the Security Council and the idea of there being a responsibility to respond to core crimes:

> The Charter gives the Security Council a wide degree of latitude to determine the most appropriate course of action. The Council should continue to respond flexibly to the demands of protecting populations from crimes and violations relating to RtoP.[6]

These tenets were largely found in earlier iterations of R2P – in the High Level Panel on Threats, Challenges and Change of 2004;[7] the Secretary General's Report entitled 'In Larger Freedom' of 2005;[8] and finally by the General Assembly at the World Summit of 2005. The Outcome Document, adopted by consensus in the Assembly in 2005 and, therefore, constituting the most authoritative understanding of

---

4 UNSC 6498 meeting (2011).

5 See UNSC Res 1199 (1998); SC Res 1203 (1998). Neither resolution expressly authorised 'necessary measures' to protect civilians in Kosovo.

6 UNSG, 'Responsibility to Protect: Timely and Decisive Response', UN Doc A/66/874-S/2012/578 (2012), para 54.

7 Report of the Secretary General's High Level Panel on Threats, Challenges and Change, 'A More Secure World' (UN 2004) recommendation 53–6.

8 UNSG, 'In Larger Freedom: Towards, Security, Development and Freedom for All' (UN, 2005) recommendation 7(b).

R2P, recited the responsibility of each individual state to protect their populations from genocide, war crimes, ethnic cleansing and crimes against humanity. It then recounted the responsibility of the international community to use diplomatic, humanitarian and other peaceful means, in accordance with Chapters VI and VIII of the Charter, to help protect populations from the above acts. Any collective action under Chapter VII was envisaged as being taken through the Security Council 'on a case-by-case basis', in cooperation with relevant regional organisations, should peaceful means prove inadequate.[9]

This 'case-by-case' approach can be used to explain and defend the different reactions of the Security Council to Libya in 2011 and Syria in 2011–2013 when crimes against humanity were being committed in both. Of course it is easier to criticise the Security Council for failing to act in the case of Syria in 2012–2013, when it acted so decisively to authorise the use of force against Libya in 2011, but the different perceptions of the threat within the permanent membership disabled it even from performing its most basic diplomatic function.

The obvious weakness in placing a responsibility to respond to specific acts of violence on a body in which a veto by any permanent member can block any effective action leads to the question of whether there are alternative legitimate and lawful configurations of states that can fulfil the R2P on behalf of the international community. In other words, when the Security Council is deadlocked in the face of imminent and catastrophic violence then other legitimate security communities should be able to act to authorise necessary measures to stop the atrocities and prevent further violence. This very much goes to the future development of both the normative and institutional facets of international conflict and security law.

8.4   Future directions

The rules on the use of force are undergoing adaptation to bring them into line with current threats, from terrorism, from cyber-attacks and from old foes like pirates, but clarification is essential. As a response to terrorist threats, the response to 9/11 has proved to be an uncertain precedent. Responding to imminent attacks by terrorists groups appears to be accepted as lawful, but a disproportionate response that

---

9 UNGA Res 60/1 (2005) paras 138–9.

not only hits the terrorists but also the host state is of dubious legality, unless it can be proven that the host state is substantially involved in the terrorist attacks themselves. Similarly, caution has to be exercised in relation to cyber-attacks where only the most serious should be seen as violations of the *jus ad bellum*. While the adaptation of the rules on the use of force to new factual or technological conditions is inevitable in any dynamic legal order, the underlying purposes of the rules on the use of force – to prevent or reduce escalation of conflicts – must not be forgotten. Similarly, in the area of threats from WMD, while it is necessary to allow a threatened state some limited degree of anticipa-tion if it is not to be annihilated, the law cannot be stretched beyond *The Caroline* criteria of having to show the 'necessity of self-defence, instant, overwhelming leaving no choice of means and no moment for deliberation' if we are to prevent conflicts from escalating. To permit states to use force first against a perceived threat that has not material-ised in an imminent attack would be to allow first strikes to become the norm, leading to devastating and escalating conflicts.

The emergence of non-state armed groups as significant actors in the use of force leads to numerous problems concerning the responsibility of both state and non-state actors. The difficulty in holding non-state actors to account under an international legal order that is still state-dominated, means that focus remains on state responsibility. This not only covers terrorist groups and the issue of when the host state is responsible for harbouring them, but also to corporate security actors. When states contract with PMSCs for the delivery of security services in post-conflict or hostile environments, the question arises as to when the contracting state (or indeed the host or home state) can be deemed responsible. It has been argued that whereas it is difficult to impute the wrongful acts of non-state actors such as PMSCs to states, those states still have obligations of due diligence, whereby they should ensure that PMSCs comply with relevant international laws. Developing the con-cept of state due diligence to cover other non-state armed actors, for example, in the case of the host state of armed insurgents, might prove to be the way forward for international law. Of course, international law should also be expanded to cover a broader range of subjects to include corporate actors so that they too directly carry obligations.

Not only does international conflict and security's normative regimes require adaptation to match rapid technological and societal changes, so too does the institutional architecture. The centrality of the UN Security Council is both a source of potential power and a serious weakness. The Council's abilities as a forum for diplomacy, its most basic function, arguably need greater attention than its military capabilities. Indeed, its competence to authorise military action is so dependent upon willing states' military capabilities that it is difficult to see how the availability and effectiveness of UN military action can be significantly improved. If the Security Council fails to adapt, for instance, to protect vulnerable populations from core crimes being committed against them, then responsibility should pass to alternative security communities – certainly the UN General Assembly has this competence and, arguably, so do legitimate regional organisations when acting within their competence. International law should empower these communities while also acting as a constraint on abuse of power by organisations and by states purporting to act in their name.

Although much debate is to be found on the complexities of the classification of armed conflicts, it is the reciprocal basis of the laws of war that requires some reconsideration so that the law, and this applies to many aspects of international conflict and security law, is underpinned by greater enforcement. Limited enforcement is provided by international criminal tribunals but, although these provide some measure of deterrence, their function is mainly to deliver retrospective justice against a limited number of war criminals. What is needed is on-going supervision, and other compliance mechanisms, which, in the area of international humanitarian law, cannot be provided by the ICRC, whose legitimacy depends on it treading a neutral line as much as possible. The possibility, mentioned in Chapter 6, of states making greater efforts to achieve collective agreement on compliance methods in the law of armed conflict is to be welcomed but it is long overdue considering that modern international humanitarian law dates from the mid-nineteenth century.

A move towards greater use of compliance mechanisms, by state reporting, by review, and by non-forcible (and exceptionally forcible) measures will also have to be balanced by increased accountability and responsibility in the area of international conflict and security law. The UN and other security communities do investigate and report on their own failures, for instance on the UN's failure to prevent genocides in Rwanda in 1994 and Srebrenica in 1995,[10] and for the sexual

---

10 Report of the Independent Inquiry into the Actions of the United Nations during the 1994 Genocide in Rwanda, UN Doc S/1999/1257 (1999); Report of the Secretary General Pursuant to General Assembly Resolution 53/35: The Fall of Srebrenica UN Doc A/54/549 (1999).

abuse committed by its peacekeepers in the DRC.[11] However, there is a lack of judicial and non-judicial mechanisms at the international level whereby victims of violations of the law can bring their claims. In relation to the UN there are scattered remedial mechanisms such as the *ad hoc* claims boards established within peacekeeping operations, the UN Compensation Commission set up to remedy the victims of Iraq's invasion and occupation of Kuwait in 1990–1991, or the ombudsperson established to review complaints about wrongful listing under the Council's targeted sanctions against al-Qaeda and the Taliban; but the lack of systematic access to justice at the international level will have to be addressed as the legal order develops. Until this develops, individuals will be forced to seek justice for violations of international conflict and security law before national courts,[12] or at the regional level,[13] where there is no guarantee that they will have *locus standi*.

11 Zeid Report, 'A comprehensive strategy to eliminate future sexual exploitation and abuse in United Nations peacekeeping operations', UN Doc A/59/710 (2005).

12 *Netherlands v Nuhanovic*, Judgment of the Supreme Court of the Netherlands, 12/03324, 6 September 2013.

13 *Kadi Yassin Abdullah an Al Barakaat International Foundations v. Council and Commission*, Joined Cases C-402/05 P and C-415/05 P, European Court of Justice Judgment, 3 September 2008; *Nada v Switzerland*, Application No. 24833/94 (1999), European Court of Human Rights Judgment, 12 September 2012.

Index